ALL EARS

PETER SZENDY

*THE AESTHETICS OF
ESPIONAGE*

ALL EARS

Translated by Roland Végső

FORDHAM UNIVERSITY PRESS)) NEW YORK)) 2017

This book was first published in French as *Sur Écoute: Esthétique de l'espionage*
by Peter Szendy © Les Éditions de Minuit, 2007.

This book's publication was supported by a subvention from the University of
Nebraska College of Arts and Sciences.

Fordham University Press has no responsibility for the persistence or
accuracy of URLs for external or third-party Internet websites referred to in
this publication and does not guarantee that any content on such websites is,
or will remain, accurate or appropriate.

Fordham University Press also publishes its books in a variety of electronic
formats. Some content that appears in print may not be available in
electronic books.

Visit us online at www.fordhampress.com.

Library of Congress Cataloging-in-Publication Data

Names: Szendy, Peter, author.
Title: All ears : the aesthetics of espionage / Peter Szendy ; translated by
    Roland Végső.
Other titles: Sur écoute. English
Description: First edition | New York, NY : Fordham University Press, 2017. |
    Includes bibliographical references.
Identifiers: LCCN 2016015036 | ISBN 9780823273959 (cloth : alk. paper) |
ISBN 9780823273966 (pbk. : alk. paper)
Subjects: LCSH: Espionage. | Aesthetics. | Music—Philosophy and aesthetics.
    | Motion pictures—Aesthetics. | Opera.
Classification: LCC BH301.E77 S9413 2017 | DDC 327.12—dc23
LC record available at https://lccn.loc.gov/2016015036

Printed in the United States of America

19 18 17   5 4 3 2 1

First edition

CONTENTS

(No) More Ears: A Preface
to the English-Language Edition

All Ears was never intended to be simply a book about current
events.

The question "Are they listening to me?"—with which, in
2007, I opened this second volume of a diptych devoted to
listening[1]—has no doubt always resonated in the hollow of
our ears as the very question that opens and orients them.[2]
For what is at stake in it is quite simply the ear of the other
that precedes mine.

However, on the path that I decided to follow in order to
resume my otological inquiries in the direction of their most
immediately ethical and political stakes, we encounter a
number of events that marked, at the time when I was writing, a profound and massive transformation of the auditory
landscape in which we deliver ourselves to this seemingly so
passive and pacific activity: hearing. These were the then
recent revelations in Europe about the Echelon network, an
inheritance of the Cold War. Since then, this transformation
has only intensified and become more evident in a new space
(that we could call "post-Snowdenian") where a generalized
otographic surveillance appears to have definitively sanc-
tioned the reign of one of James Joyce's obscure characters:

Earwicker, an emblem of those "big ears" to which we are exposed every second of our lives in the (cyber) world.

The NSA spying on Angela Merkel's phone conversations and on those of two French ministers; Edward Snowden seeking asylum in Russia; user data collected on Google, Facebook, YouTube, Skype: We could all continue the list of facts exposed by the *Guardian*, the *Washington Post*, or *Le Monde*, a list that keeps growing every day. The methods are more and more sophisticated (without knowing anything about them, we have all heard of the surveillance program Prism and the computer system XKeyscore): Espionage has become digital, and as such, to use Deleuze's term, it obeys the logic of control rather than that of disciplinary surveillance to the extent that listening, as a particular sense or sensorial region that can be identified in its difference, appears to dissolve itself in the generalized indexation and machinic auscultation of communication flows. But the wager of this book is that perhaps the paradigm of auditory espionage (this old paradigm to which Earwicker gives his name) allows us better than any other to understand what is happening to us, even if this paradigm appears to be already a thing of the past. It is as if there were more and more ears— only ears, everywhere—even though there are no real ears anymore.

In the face of this simultaneously omnipresent and evasive actuality or virtuality (which constitute the very stakes of what I call, after and following the panopticism described by Foucault, panacousticism), the basic gesture of *All Ears* was above all archaeological. The book tried to think the epochs and stratifications of *overhearing*, as well as the genesis of the otological surplus that constitutes it. But the genealogy was shadowed by an apparently contrary or irreconcilable inquiry that concerned the structure rather than the history of auditory espionage: The possibility of this perversion that inhabits listening from the very beginning appeared to me to be what, at the same time, also *makes it possible*. It is in this sense that the subtitle of the book, *The Aesthetics of Espionage*, alludes to the figure of the spy simultaneously as a motif or theme in (cinematic, literary, and musical) works of art (in short, in "aesthetic" productions in the common usage of the word), but also as the condition of the possibility of listening in general: Espionage (the ear of the other) could then be understood also and above all in the sense of what we could call, slightly deflecting the Kant of the *Critique of Pure Reason*, a "transcendental aesthetic" of aurality.

In the end, however, I refrained from putting things in these terms, since the word "transcendental" was not quite right. Rather, we are dealing with something "quasi-transcendental" (as Derrida put it, to whom the book is dedicated in the form of a posthumous homage). Engaged in what is considered to be the (second) oldest profession in the world, the spy forms a part of a (historical or empirical) series of figures of listening. It is one term or one element in the series. At the same time, however, it also accounts for the cause or the possibility of the very series to which it belongs.[3] Today I would perhaps no longer say this using the same vocabulary, but this was what dictated to me the choice of the subtitle at the time when I was writing *All Ears*.

Another reason to doubt the good old Kantian term "transcendental" is that if it is true that espionage makes listening possible, at the same time it also makes it impossible. What puts in motion the drive toward surveillance, through which listening becomes the listening that it is, happens to be also what inhibits it and makes it deaf (as I show through Orpheus and Kafka's story "The Burrow").[4] The political consequences of this structure extend everywhere today, to the United States as well as to France: When we try to hear everything, we do not hear anything.

All Ears, therefore, is fundamentally a book about impossible listening. About overhearing as something that is *possible only as impossible.*

It is on the basis of this auditory aporia that we will see emerge here, I hope, the true stakes that sustain these pages in their urgency (which is not simply their topicality): the question of a *responsibility of listening*, as I outlined it already in *Listen: A History of Our Ears.* The reader will find here its necessary further development.

Translator's Note

The translation of philosophy is often confounded by the simple fact that philosophical writings tend to explicitly anticipate the terms of their own translatability. Even if the problem of translation is not explicitly thematized in the original text, the conceptual work performed in it can often be extended to the theory and practice of translation as well. In these cases, it might appear as if the original wanted to control its own translation by defining in advance a theory of translation that it considers to be the most appropriate to its own arguments. This is certainly true of Peter Szendy's *Sur Écoute,* for it would be difficult to come up with a more appropriate metaphor for the act of translation than the central concept elaborated by the book in the form of the philosophical neologism *surécoute.* To put it differently, Szendy's text invites us to read and translate it through this new concept of *overhearing* that, at least potentially, inscribes the act of translation in the long series of possible figures for the act of listening.

The translator, therefore, becomes a spy listening in on other people's conversations. Following Szendy's argument, then, we would have to consider the possibility that translation, as an act of overhearing, is caught in the same aporetic structures as listening. The desire to translate, to translate it all, in full vigilance over all the nuances of the original, is a panoptic and panacoustic desire for mastery. Without this desire, translation would not get under way. But this drive produces an excess of translation that eventually turns translation against itself. This would be the work of the death drive inhibiting translation: The desire to translate it all threatens to turn into the staging of the impossibility of translation.

So what are we supposed to hear in this translation of Szendy's work? The ultimate surprise of Szendy's book is that it once again turns the translation of a seemingly simple term, *écoute*, into a genuine challenge. What appears to be a most translatable French word (that would invite merely an automatic direct substitution) in the end turns out to be something that cannot be translated without mobilizing the secret underground reserves of the target language. One of the stakes of Szendy's work is to make this simple term once again resist translation with a new intensity. This resistance, then, becomes an occasion for the English speaker to reflect on the vocabulary of listening with a renewed alertness.

Szendy relies on two essential moves to achieve this goal: etymology and a deliberate deployment of semantic ambiguity. First, through an etymological analysis, Szendy expands the meaning of the term *écoute* to include a whole set of new associations. Today, this word is most often used either to refer to the act of listening in general or to auditory surveillance (for example, in the form of wiretapping). But Szendy expands this field of associations by evoking unheard-of nuances: a place from which it is possible to hear other people's conversations; a person (like a nun at a convent) who listens in on other people's conversations; a guard or a sentinel who monitors the enemy's progress. The archaic meanings are revived in these pages and brought to life again only to haunt our understanding of listening like ghosts and revenants. In their haunting, they all point toward the same conclusion: Listening and spying appear to be structurally connected.

In addition to the etymological expansion, the English translation must also reckon with the complications introduced by the French reflexive pronoun in *s'écouter*. As the conclusion of the book also makes clear, the core of Szendy's argument could be described as a transposition from the visual to the auditory field of Jacques Derrida's reflections on the semantic complications of the phrase *se regarder*. In other words, Szendy translates Derrida as well. The reader of the English translation is, therefore, asked to survey the text with a heightened acoustic sense for the possibilities of listening. Every time terms of listening, hearing, and surveillance appear in the text, we need to remember that a single generative semantic matrix unites them all: *écoute*. The two strategies work together, on the one hand, to inscribe the history of the word *écoute* in the history of espionage and surveillance and, on the other, to suspend the fantasy of the simple subject-object or self-other relation at the heart of listening. The word "listening" is now called upon to account for the encounter with the "ear of the other" in the hollow of our own ears: Listening names the uncontrollable movements of reciprocity and self-reflexivity between self and other in ways that undermine classical topologies of hearing.

This forcing of the meaning of *écoute*, therefore, leads us to a theory of an excessive form of listening, *surécoute*. Ultimately, it is the translation of Szendy's new concept (which doubles as a metaphor for translation) that illustrates most clearly the problems at hand. The significant point for the act of translation is that this is the passage in which Szendy's text most explicitly engages the problem of translation. In what sense can we say that "overhearing" is a translation of *surécoute*? First of all, as Szendy himself suggests, his French neologism is in fact an attempt to fill a lexical hiatus in French.

It is as if the French language had met one of its historical limits here, and the task of the philosopher is to produce a new word to fill in a hole. How is this task accomplished? Szendy literally translates (in the form of a calque) the English word "overhearing" into French as *surécoute*. Thus, translation is at the core of the issues evoked by the concept of *surécoute*.

Yet the mere fact that *surécoute* is presented to us as the translation of "overhearing" does not necessarily imply that this is a reversible relation. It might appear counterintuitive, but we must remember that it is not self-evident that "overhearing" is in fact a translation of *surécoute*. For what is lost in the reverse translation (when we translate into English *surécoute* as "overhearing") is the fact that the French is a neologism whose meaning is defined by Szendy's argument. In English, the word "overhearing" already brings with it a complex set of meanings and associations that predate Szendy's invention of the French term. Thus, translating *surécoute* as "overhearing" threatens to delete the calculated strangeness of the original. On first sight, there is nothing strange about the English word. So, in order to repeat the gesture of Szendy's literalizing act of translation that produces a neologism, the translator might have to consider new possibilities: For example, one option would have been to translate *surécoute* as "overlistening" in order to preserve this strangeness.

But in the end, this solution does not suffice either. Our task is precisely to hear and even overhear in Szendy's usage of the English term "overhearing" the French *surécoute*. After Szendy's work is done, overhearing is not the same word that it used to be. The strangeness of overhearing comes from Szendy's reinterpretation of the prefix "over" that no longer exclusively designates a spatial relation but is now also a sign of an excess (as in the English word "overinterpretation"). Like an insidious mole, the word *surécoute* undermines the meaning of the English term "overhearing" as the effects of this translation inscribe their alterity in the economy of the same. It is only in this sense that we can say that "overhearing" is a translation of *surécoute*. So when Szendy translates "overhearing" as *surécoute*, we encounter what I would like to call a genuine event of translation: The new word created by this act of translation simultaneously changes the source and target languages. Out of the nothingness of the French lacuna, something is created that restructures the whole field.

The translation of *All Ears*, therefore, encounters an inherent limit of translation when it discovers that the original already translates (itself). The logic of Szendy's argument suggests that the problem of translation is best expressed, once again forcing the possibilities of the French language, by the reflexive verb *se traduire*: The original itself translates (from English to French) and, at the same time, it translates itself (from French into English). Therefore, the source language and the target language enter into relations of mutual translation: They translate each other. This state of mutual translations, an inextricable dynamism between the same and the other, is the real condition of translation.

So the reader of this translation is invited to participate in this game of listening and espionage. Szendy's neologisms (of which *surécoute* is only one example) aim to reinvent the language of listening itself and, this way, ask the reader to implement the very theory expounded on these pages within the practice of reading itself. Thus, the task of reading here is to listen for the hidden noise of the other's murmur masked by the rumble of translation without giving in to the temptation of full mastery. This practice constitutes the politics of listening as well as the politics of translation.

The moment he thinks he is being watched, he starts singing.

—*The Testament of Dr. Mabuse*

Entrance: The Spies of Jericho

Are they listening to me?

Do they hear me? Do they receive me? Do they spy on me when I speak? When I confide secrets? When I share an idea or an opinion?

That is not possible—I tell myself as I try to reason with myself. Why would they keep me under surveillance like that? There is surely nothing that could lead me to believe that I am being listened to—that I am being *overheard*?

Of course, reading the newspapers, I encounter the recurrent and often disquieting signs of the unheard-of development that auditory surveillance seems to be undergoing in its most violently arbitrary forms. These include the phone-tapping scandals in the Élysée Palace under Mitterrand's presidency, whose trials are in full swing as I am writing now, and more recently, the one that targeted the former Secretary-General of the United Nations, Kofi Annan.[1] Or consider the case of "Echelon," the system of espionage that could allegedly intercept any communication circulating in the world. Created in 1947 by the United States and Great Britain, Echelon is a network born of the Cold War that the

American National Security Agency reinvented during the nineties for civilian and economic purposes.[2]

Relying on an expression that has already entered journalistic language, we often use the term "big ears" to refer to radars and other instruments of reception that constitute this ever-growing network of listening and this auditory web. Seeing them, I confess that I sometimes shudder thinking that they can hear me as well. And I am not alone in this. Far from it, since a certain *fantasy of listening* has by now installed or implanted itself just as much in our daily gestures as in our political reality.

Where does this fantasy come from that haunts our fictive as well as real situations? Whether it emerges in our lives or in our stories, from where does it draw its haunting force?

For a while now, I have been avidly reading everything that I could about spies. In fact, I feel a bit like Robert Redford's character in *Three Days of the Condor*, who passes his time in an obscure office connected to the CIA analyzing with the help of a computer books and novels that he receives from all over the world to try to discover in them hidden or coded messages. Until that fateful day when, without knowing it, he puts his finger on a secret hidden and buried under a literary cover, and he finds himself involved in the hell of a plot that completely overwhelms him.

As I am hunting for spies wherever I believe I might be able to find them described or depicted (in films, in operas, in books), will I end up meeting them in real life?

I lock my door and plunge back into my reading.

It was, indeed, with feverish curiosity that I ripped open the big envelope in which my order had arrived: *The Ultimate Spy Book*, an illustrated history of espionage that also resembles a manual for the apprentice secret agent.[3] The cover is lurid, flashy, and filled with images of gadgets worthy of the worst films of the genre. Even worse: As I leaf through the book, I discover two forewords on facing pages, one signed by an ex-director of the CIA and the other by a retired general of the KGB. Of course, this way the work gains in authority. The foreword written by the American goes so far as to describe the author, Keith Melton, as "perhaps the world's most outstanding collector of, and expert in, intelligence equipment."[4] But the rhetoric has something immodest about it. With the end of the Cold War, we read, "Now that the United States and Russia are no longer enemies," the task is to present a common front against "terrorists, purveyors of ethnic and religious hatred, nuclear proliferators, and crime and drug lords."[5]

I admit that I am a bit ashamed of this new addition to my library. But this is one of the rare sources of intelligence that I could find about the necessarily secret world of intelligence.

The Russian author of the other foreword catches my attention when he writes: "Spying . . . has often been called 'the second oldest profession.' . . . Intelligence-gathering was transformed by satellites, lasers, computers, and other gadgetry capable of ferreting out secrets from every corner of the globe."[6] What would be, then, the age of this profession whose technological apparatuses and prostheses have recently undergone such momentous changes? How deep has this practice of listening and surveillance that espionage is cast its roots? In its secondary position, in its relation of mythical or phantasmatic succession with regard to what we believe to be the absolutely first profession in the world, what acquisitions of what immemorial secrets could it hold in reserve for us?

The author of the book, the expert and collector H. Keith Melton, devotes a short chapter to the ancient history of this "profession": "Around 500 BC, the ancient Chinese strategist Sun Tzu wrote about the importance of intelligence and espionage networks in his classic book *The Art of War*. The Bible contains more than a hundred references to spies and intelligence-gathering. Most elements of modern espionage, however, originated in 15th- and 16th-century Europe."[7]

This is all he says of the prehistory of espionage—and that is not much. Sun Tzu, for example, already proposed a remarkable typology of espionage when he distinguished "five sorts of secret agents" who are called the "treasure of the sovereign": "Native agents are those of the enemy's country people whom we employ.... Inside agents are enemy officials whom we employ.... Doubled agents are enemy spies whom we employ.... Expendable agents are those of our own spies who are deliberately given fabricated information.... Living agents are those who return with information."[8]

As for the Bible, we can find in it quite a few references to spies. But in addition to the great number of occurrences of the word itself, a superficial survey of Louis Segond's classic translation, for example, provided me with the following piece of information that is especially relevant for me: The famous episode of the wall of Jericho in the book of Joshua is not merely a story about the power of sound but also an affair involving moles.

Joshua "secretly" dispatches two men as "spies" to explore the Promised Land, "especially Jericho" (Josh. 2:1).[9] They spend the night at the house of a prostitute called Rahab. She hides them on her roof when the king of Jericho, who gets wind of their arrival, sends his men to search for them. In exchange, they promise to spare her life. Later, the priests accompanying Joshua, obeying divine instructions, blow their deafening trumpets. And the shout of the people provoked by this signal brings down the walls of the city (Josh. 6:20). The spies keep their promise: During the capture of the city, in the middle of what we imagine to be a great massacre,

Rahab and her family are the only ones spared ("Her family lived in Israel ever since. For she hid the messengers whom Joshua sent to spy out Jericho." [Josh. 6:25]).

How should we read this old spy story? How should we interpret this testamentary alliance between the two "oldest professions in the world," working together to form a secret pocket of resistance, a cryptic enclave protected against the crushing power of an invasion launched in the form of a shout or a resounding flood?

I see an allegory here. Not, as it is usually believed, an allegory of the pure power of sound in itself (does it even exist, by the way, without ears to hear it?), but rather an allegory of the way sound *is listened to*.[10]

Everything happened as if Joshua's agents, dispatched and sent off to the outposts in order to proceed to a preliminary auscultation of the terrain, had somehow anticipated by their listening the shouting of the people. As if they had been the vanguard of the phonic wave that was destined to destroy the ramparts in a movement that, in league with those inside, had also conserved a space subtracted from the power that they represented: They had prepared for the capture of Jericho and the massacre of its people all the while they preserved Rahab and her family.

Thus, moving beyond the surface of the kind of rigid exegesis that can see in this story nothing but the pure force of the destructive power of the propagation of sound, this biblical episode could actually also allow to resonate within this force, based on the anticipatory movement of a precursory listening, something that would actually preempt it. That is to say, in an apparently inseparable manner, something that would precede this force, prepare it, or clear its path by being at the breaking point of its wave; and something that would, at the same time, limit it, contain it, would form an obstacle to what is absolutely overflowing or immeasurable in it. In short, what appears to accompany the power of sound here, as it announces itself to listening and precedes itself in it, is a double movement of simultaneous facilitation and preemption. Borrowing from a certain military vocabulary that will often return in the course of these pages, we could say that the listening of the pioneers who are Joshua's spies is a work of drilling in the service of a victorious shout that listening also undermines in its absolute power. It is, thus, as if a kind of double agent were implanted in listening in the form of a tension toward the breaking of a phonic wave to come.[11]

Wouldn't there be, then, from the very beginning a basic structural affinity between listening and espionage? And if, going beyond mere topicality, every listener is perhaps primarily and above all a spy, isn't it in this immemorial collusion that we should search for the powers of listening both resisting and siding with power?

Reading or interpreting the listener as a mole—a motif whose historical and political necessity will gradually emerge here—is, however, not simply a catchphrase. As Du Mu (the famous Chinese poet from the ninth century) suggests in his commentary on the thirteenth chapter of Sun Tzu's treatise, especially through the figure of the double agent, the spy and espionage constantly provoke doubling, duplicity, and duplication. Considering the case when "the enemy sends an ambassador to us," Du Mu advises that we should "charge someone with the task of living close to him in order to observe his reactions." But this first agent immediately calls for another: "While the emissary is day and night intimate with his companion [the ambassador], I will charge a man with a trained ear to listen to their conversations as he hides behind a thick *double* wall."[12]

Everything appears to redouble itself: from the agent to the partition or the wall itself that hides the agent as he, at the same time, crosses this wall by means of his listening. This repeated reduplication in and of listening is what is going to be at stake here.

Discipline and Listen

Before the Wiretap

Spies listen. Of course, they also look in order to keep watch over things. But an important part of their activities involves listening. As Chia Lin, one of the commentators of *The Art of War*, writes: "An army without secret agents is exactly like a man without eyes or ears."[1]

Spies, therefore, are usually listening. They are, above all, attentive listeners to what is afoot. They are hearing devices deployed to capture what is coming or what is hiding, or what is secretly coming. Espionage, thus, appears to be one of the oldest known practices of listening to the world or of the auscultation of the world.

At the same time, however, isn't there an urge toward spying in every listening? Does not listening always participate in a work of *intelligence*, as one says in English?

If it should turn out to be the case that listening and espionage inextricably implicated each other in their respective histories, it would become difficult to keep count of, to determine the number of, or to circumscribe the actions and passions of spies, these remarkable listeners, in the Bible or elsewhere.

Even without raising possible issues of translation, it should be clear that, no matter how thorough it might be, a mere survey of the literal occurrences of the terms that designate and reveal them in plain sight ("spy," "secret agent," "rat" or "snitch," "sycophant," "informer," "snoop," "spook," etc.) would not suffice to flush out all the moles with "big ears" hiding in the tunnels of all the different texts and archives. Could we go as far as thinking, for example, that the very first listeners, Adam and Eve, were not far from adopting the role of spies when, after having sinned by tasting the fruit of the "tree of the knowledge of good and evil," they hide and seem to listen anxiously for the "sound" of the footsteps (or the voice, according to some other versions) of the Eternal who walks in the garden at the fall of night? (Gen. 3:8).[2] The first human listening—Edenic or Adamic audition—is in any case, using Roland Barthes's words from an essay that we will have to reread here, oriented "to certain indices."[3]

I can, of course, only dream and speculate about these first fantastic and phantasmatic ears. However, an intelligence operation with the code name *écoute* properly conducted through etymological networks provides me with a whole number of other reasons for speculation.[4]

In 1694, the *Dictionnaire de l'Académie française* gave the following definition for the verb *escouter*: "to hear with attention, to lend an ear in order to hear." Strangely enough, however, the noun *escoute* does not refer to the simple and neutral action corresponding to this verb. It means: "place from which one listens *without being seen*" (emphasis added). Listening, in its French history at least, must have first meant the posts and outposts where one hides in order to catch what is being said. Or, by way of an adjectival apposition, it must have named the ones who practice auditory surveillance: In fact, the same dictionary mentions that a *sœur escoute* is "the nun given as an assistant to someone who goes to the parlor in order to hear [*escouter*] what is being said in the conversation."

These old related meanings, that undeniably turn listening into an affair of spies, have maintained themselves in their ramifications until much later to the exclusion of all others. The article on "Listening" in Diderot and d'Alembert's *Encyclopedia* laconically states only the following: "This is what they call in architecture the latticed galleries in public schools where people retire *who do not want to be seen*." And the big *Larousse* of the mid-nineteenth century, after citing the previous definition by the Academy, indicates still other similar usages that appear to bring listening even closer to an activity of intelligence:

> A closed place in a convent, from which one can follow the service without seeing or being seen.

> *Military*. Small mineshaft from which one can hear if the enemy miner is working or advancing. // Guards placed in these tunnels to follow the progress of the enemy's work.

Without a doubt, in its French etymology, listening must have first been an affair of moles.

Overhearing and Diaphony

Sur écoute: as they say it in French, written as two separate words, of someone—a politician, a criminal, an undesirable or too nosy journalist—who is put under surveillance, who is being spied upon. *Mettre* or *placer sur écoute* means to have someone's phone tapped.

But, written as one word, the neologism *surécoute* could be understood as an intensification of listening, as its hyperbolic form, taken to incandescence, to its most extreme and most active point. In short, *surécoute* as a synonym for auditory hyperesthesia, a superlative super-listening.[5]

Furthermore, *surécoute* appears to be a literal calque of the wonderful English expression *overhearing*.[6]

To overhear: an activity that many of Shakespeare's characters, for example, indulge in. They spy on each other. They open their ears to hear something far or close that is always at the distance of a secret.[7] In *A Midsummer Night's Dream*, Oberon declares that he is invisible and that he will "overhear" a conversation (2.1.561). But it is in *Hamlet* above all that we are invited to a grand staging of overhearing as a form of auditory indiscretion.

The motif is announced by the first words of the ghost: "Mark me," he tells Hamlet before revealing to him that "the whole ear of Denmark / Is by a forged process of my death / Rankly abused" (1.5.773–75). The father's ghost—who, by the way, died because of the poison that was poured "in the porches of [his] ears"—demands to be heard by his son. This means that he wants to be literally marked or remarked: "Mark me" (1.5.734). The same verb, the same verbal mark will designate later the way Polonius intends to survey Hamlet's behavior in Ophelia's presence: He tells the queen and the king to "mark the encounter" (2.2.1266). It is as "lawful espials," "seeing, [yet] unseen," that they prepare to overhear the conversation of the unhappy lovers (3.1.1719–20).

But since the exchange did not produce any convincing clues, Polonius proposes that this time, after the play within the play, Hamlet should be left alone with his mother so that he will reveal himself to her: "POLONIUS: And I'll be placed, so please you, in the ear / Of all their conference" (3.1.1876). Meanwhile, during the play that the actors put on at Hamlet's demand, the latter charges Horatio with surveying the reactions of the usurper who killed his father: "Observe mine uncle" (3.2.1959). Thus, we who are watching the play within the play (whose title is *The Mousetrap*) are also about to see a spectator (Horatio) in the process of spying on another character, the king. The *mise en abyme* of observation matches here the structure of narrative framing: the surveillance of the royal audience member trapped by this theater within the theater is preceded by the encounter between Hamlet and Ophelia (themselves surveyed by Polonius and the king), and is followed by the conversation between Hamlet and the queen (which is also being overheard).

In fact, Polonius tells the king who has lost his composure while witnessing the representation of his crime:

> My lord, he's going to his mother's closet:
> Behind the arras I'll convey myself,
> To hear the process; . . .
> And, as you said, and wisely was it said,
> 'Tis meet that some more audience than a mother,
> Since nature makes them partial, should o'erhear
> The speech, of vantage. . . . (3.3.2307–13)

Listening "of vantage," listening by redoubling the listening of another, also means (as the English version suggests) to hear more and better: its additional *advantage* is that it is in a position "of vantage." At the same time, it also means to hear *in advance*, like a spy who positions himself at the outpost or the advance-guard of what is happening in order to *prevent* what is coming. In this sense, according to an apparent paradox, overhearing, as an excessive listening that adds itself by way of a surfeit, concerns also immediately a *prehearing*: As in the case of the spies of Jericho, we are dealing with an auditory prevention of what is happening.

In short, *Hamlet* could be inscribed into the infinite collection of spy stories. That is to say, stories about *moles*, according to the name given to the ghost when he descends under the stage to repeat in the form of an echo the words of his son. "Ghost cries under the stage," the stage directions state right before Hamlet, emphasizing the ubiquity of the paternal specter ("Hic et ubique?"), addresses him in the following terms: "Well said, old mole! canst work i' the earth so fast? / A worthy pioneer!" (1.5.915–16). The ghost, like the other characters of *Hamlet*, appears to be a watchman in the underground tunnels of the text: Just like a listening guard (as it was defined by the *Larousse* dictionary in the nineteenth century), he is a pioneer, a soldier who is digging in order to overhear what is going on.

Several opera characters also participate in the act of overhearing.

This is what Monostatos does in Mozart's *The Magic Flute* when he hides himself in order to hear what the Queen of the Night and her daughter, Pamina, talk about (II, 8): "Ha! We must overhear [*belauschen*] that from a distance." This is what Cherubino does in *The Marriage of Figaro* when he finds himself obliged to retire behind a chair so that he will not be seen by the Count and, therefore, witnesses the scene when the latter tries to seduce Susanna (I, 6).

I will lend an attentive ear to these spying characters, these overhearers, who present themselves to us, the audience, who in turn listen to them during the performance of the opera. I will try to capture what the music gives us to understand of their listening: namely, of their actions or passions as listeners, but also of their places or positions within the work when they are listening. So much so that, just as in *Hamlet* and the situation described by Du Mu, once again there will be a surfeit of ears, a surplus of the web of listening.

Overhearing, then, appears to name or evoke a certain proliferating polyphony of listening: multiple *lines of listening*— in the sense of telephone lines—that are connected, redouble themselves, interfere with each other, and sometimes get blurred. The English word *overhearing* does share this technical or technological connotation: In the field of telecommunication, it designates what in French is called *diaphonie*, namely a defect in transmission caused by the transfer of a signal, channel, or a line onto another. A superposition of voices, the interference of another, secondary line with the primary one. When we hear strange voices from another conversation over the phone or when some alien music interferes with a recording.

Listening, overhearing, interference, diaphony: In this linguistic Babel, in this maze of archives where I am searching for the word, the watchword, the keyword in order to name what promises to be a campaign of intelligence concerning the patent or latent relations between listening and power, I find myself at a crossroads where several paths open up which I will follow one after the other like a detective. Or sometimes simultaneously, dispatching several agents at the same time.

In its properly musical history, the word *diaphonia*, after having been assigned the meaning of "dissonance" by ancient Greek theoreticians (in opposition to *symphonia* as "consonance"), had been used in medieval treatises since the ninth century as a synonym for "polyphony." On the one hand, therefore, following this path, trying to hear in *overhearing* something like an *auditory diaphony*, our task would be to examine what a dissonant listening could be. Not the hearing of a dissonance, of a musical object awaiting some resolution in consonance, but a listening that is itself affected by *diaphonia*. That is to say, listening according to (at least) two "voices," redoubled and split in the hollow of my ears.

On the other hand, translating *overhearing* as *surécoute*, our task would be to lend an ear to the multiple resonances of this invented word in the silent ambiguity of its written form. A blank space, a pause, an interruption in its transmission could always separate its prefix from its root or base. But when we say of someone that he is *sur écoute*, in two words, this expression usually implies the interposition of a technological apparatus for the purposes of interception and, often, recording. *Être (mis) sur écoute* does not simply mean being listened to in secret with "naked ears," as Polonius, Monostatos, or Cherubino does. Overhearing as *surécoute* is inseparable from the presence of tele-technologies of listening that not only allow for a potentially infinite distance between listener and the one being listened to but are also most often tied to a phonographic archiving instrument.

These are the two traits that James Joyce brought together in one of the main characters of *Finnegans Wake*: Earwicker. The name itself functions as a kind of smashup of "wicked," "earwig," and "earwigging." Joyce writes: "Earwicker, that patternmind, that paradigmatic ear, receptoretentive as his of Dionysius."[8] Earwicker, as we can see, is equipped with a faculty of reception *and* retention thanks to which he can compile a "long list . . . of all abusive names he was called."[9] Earwicker the spy could, then, serve as an emblem of this overhearing in which reception from a distance is also immediately a form of archival retention.

A Small History of Big Ears (Toward the Panacousticon)

Earwicker's history would be a long one, a vast genealogy whose long branches reach into the present. I recall here only a few of its singular moments.

First of all, as Joyce himself suggests with his passing reference to Dionysus, there is an ancient "big ear" known as "The Ear of Dionysus" described by many travelers who had visited Syracuse.[10] Around 1780, in his travel journals from Sicily, Swinburne speaks of "a groove or a channel, which served, as is supposed, to collect the sounds that rose from the speakers below, and to convey them to a pipe in a small double cell above, where they were heard with the greatest distinctness."[11] Having carefully examined this space, Swinburne has no doubt about its purpose: It has been "constructed intentionally for a prison, and a listening place."[12]

A century before Swinburne, the Jesuit father Athanasius Kircher, in his *Musurgia universalis*, mentions Dionysus the Tyrant's mythical grotto as the first example of what he calls "echotechtonics" (an architecture of echoes) used for the purposes of auditory surveillance.[13] He also describes artificially constructed versions: no longer natural crevices but palaces and all kinds of buildings.[14]

In these buildings where speech and its secret capture are constructed simultaneously, conforming to the French etymology, the rooms or chambers devoted to *overhearing* would certainly deserve the name *écoutes*. We should mention that

(*Musurgia universalis*, t. II, p. 305)

they are located above, at a height. The spying ears dwell in the attic or the eaves (hence the English term "eavesdropping"). We are reminded of the strange and gripping story by Italo Calvino, "A King Listens," in which architectural vocabulary and the physiological description of the ear are deliberately blended: "The palace is all whorls, lobes: it is a great ear, whose anatomy and architecture trade names and functions: pavilions, ducts, shell, labyrinths. You are crouched at the bottom, in the innermost zone of the palace-ear, of your own ear; the palace is the ear of the king."[15] A list from which no doubt nothing is missing in order to complete this *architect-aural* vocabulary but the "oval window" through which the "vestibule" communicates with the middle ear.

These architectural devices, grottos, and palaces are in a certain sense the precursors in the acoustic domain of the apparatuses of surveillance that Michel Foucault called *panoptic*, borrowing a term from Jeremy Bentham's plan for an *Inspection-House* in 1787.[16]

Regardless of its exact function (prison, hospital, corrections house, or even school), the building conceived according to Bentham's plans must allow for the total and incessant visibility of its occupants: "Ideal perfection" would be achieved if "each person" could be "under the eyes" of his or her observer(s) "during every instant of time."[17] Since such a condition cannot be realized in practice, Bentham proposes that we make sure that every inmate, "seeing reason to believe as much, and not being able to satisfy himself to the contrary," should at least imagine ("conceive") that he is the object of uninterrupted vigilance.

Bentham's panoptic plan, as it is presented in the second letter for the scenario of a penitentiary, consists of a circular building: the position of the observer occupies its center, while the prison cells are located on the circumference separated from each other by the radii of the circle. In order to make sure that none of the prisoners isolated in this manner from the others will know for sure if he is in fact being watched or not, the overall plan is carefully supplemented by an apparatus that Foucault described in the following way:

> In order to make the presence or absence of the inspector unverifiable, so that the prisoners, in their cells, cannot even see a shadow, Bentham envisaged not only venetian blinds on the windows of the central observation hall, but, on the inside, partitions that intersected the hall at right angles and, in order to pass from one quarter to the other, not doors but zig-zag openings; for the slightest noise, a gleam of light, a brightness in a half-opened door would betray the presence of the guardian. The Panopticon is a machine for dissociating the see/being seen dyad: in the peripheric ring, one is totally seen, without ever seeing; in the central tower, one sees everything without ever being seen.[18]

What matters for me here is that this visual architecture, this all-seeing machine, goes hand in hand with the possibility (that Bentham envisages without truly developing) of an apparatus that we could call *panacoustic*. On two separate occasions, in the tenth and the twenty-first letters, Bentham evokes the voice and the ear. The first time around, we are dealing with the transmission of voice as an instance of authority:

> To save the troublesome exertion of voice that might otherwise be necessary, and to prevent one prisoner from knowing that the inspector was occupied by another prisoner at a distance, a small tin tube might reach from each cell to the inspector's lodge. . . . By means of this implement, the slightest whisper of the one might be heard by

the other. . . . With regard to instruction, . . . in all cases where directions, given verbally and at a distance, are sufficient, these tubes will be found of use. They will save, on the one hand, the exertion of voice it would require, on the part of the instructor, to communicate instruction to the workmen without quitting his central station in the lodge; and, on the other, the confusion which would ensue if different instructors or persons in the lodge were calling to the cells at the same time. And, in the case of hospitals, the quiet that may be insured by this little contrivance, trifling as it may seem at first sight, affords an additional advantage.[19]

What Bentham imagines here as an addition or a supplementary accessory to his Panopticon is a simultaneously pandirectional and selective megaphone of sorts: a Panacousticon that facilitates communication and transmission between observer and observed in the context of efficiently organized labor.

The second time, however, when hearing is evoked (in the final letter devoted to schools), Bentham is trying to distinguish the principle of the Panopticon from that of the ancient and outdated "ear of Dionysus":

I hope no critic of more learning than candour will do an inspection-house so much injustice as to compare it to *Dionysius' ear*. The object of that contrivance was to know what prisoners said without their suspecting any such thing. The object of the inspection principle is directly the reverse: it is to make them not only *suspect*, but be *assured*, that whatever they do is known, even though that should not be the case. Detection is the object of the first: *prevention*, that of the latter. In the former case the ruling person is a spy; in the latter he is a monitor. The object of the first was to pry into the secret recesses of the heart; the latter, confining its attention to *overt acts*, leaves thoughts and fancies to their proper *ordinary*, the court *above*.[20]

This way, the Panopticon with its potential panacoustic supplement is simultaneously more and less than the ear of Dionysus: more, because here surveillance is potentially permanent; less, because it is seemingly not aimed at the intimate secrets of its occupants.

Bentham's Panopticon as well as his Panacousticon, however, appear to be inscribed in the history of espionage, if we consider the fact that, paradoxically, the word used to distinguish them from spying (namely, the term "monitor") has turned out to be astonishingly premonitory, if I may say so. In English as well as in French, a *monitor* is of course primarily an instructor, a guide, or a trainer. But with time the word has also come to designate, due to our technological development, a surveillance device or an information system (for example, a "cardiac monitor" or a "control monitor"). It is not unthinkable that, in modern espionage, access to latent secrets becomes indistinguishable from the observation of patent actions like the ones that Bentham described. So much so that the distinction between spy and monitor becomes fragile if not impossible.

Foucault noticed the possibility of a panacoustic extension of Bentham's plan and commented on it in a footnote: "In his first version of the *Panopticon*, Bentham had also imagined an acoustic surveillance, operated by means of pipes leading from the cells to the central tower. In the *Postscript*, he abandoned the idea, perhaps because he could not introduce into it the principle of dissymmetry and prevent the prisoners from hearing the inspector as well as the inspector hearing them."[21] Foucault, however, overlooks the fact that with these steel pipes Bentham was not aiming for surveillance but rather for communication between the different orders. On the one hand, it is of course undeniable that Bentham would have had trouble trying to acoustically insulate these pipes and render them one-directional the way he could have done for the visual sunbeams by means of venetian blinds and partitions. On the other hand, however, as Kircher's engravings also demonstrate, the power of the propagation and infiltration of sound has never prevented the development of an "echotechtonics" of listening.

What, then, is at stake in the difference between hearing and seeing with regard to the necessary dissymmetry implied by intelligence understood as the acquisition or detection of a secret in general?

Before lending an ear to what the Orpheus myth could give us to understand of a certain impossible reversion, reversibility, or reciprocity, I will restrict myself here to two remarks, two clues:

1. For Bentham's plan, the problematic horizon of surveillance—whether it is auditory or visual—consists of the loopback of the apparatus over itself. It is, in fact, important for Bentham that the prisoners should be protected by their own permanent visibility, that is to say, by general transparency. So the Panopticon is conceived in such a way that the agents of surveillance are themselves put under surveillance through the inclusion of every potential visitor in the system of inspections. It is as if the necessity of a structural dissymmetry in the circulation of looks and gazes (and listening) infinitely deferred closure, the dream of a closed circuit, by incessantly injecting a surplus of eyes (and ears): in the end, what Bentham calls the "grand com-

mittee of the public" could be nothing but the *différance* of and in reciprocal pansurveillance.[22]

2. I cannot help but think here of what Freud defined, alongside the so-called "primal scene" (which is essentially of a visual or scopic nature), as a "phantasy of listening."[23] Discussing a patient who regularly believed to have heard a noise when she was in bed with her lover (she imagined that she was under surveillance or being overheard), Freud comments: "Such noises are on the contrary an indispensable part of the phantasy of listening, and they reproduce *either* the sounds which betray parental intercourse *or* those by which the listening child fears to betray itself."[24] *Either/or*: The phantasy of listening threatens in both directions. Its danger radiates from two sides: toward the scene of discovery but also toward the listener. This slight dissymmetry with regard to seeing, that is to say, this lesser protection of listening as the secret place of spying, could it have something to do with a significant lexical lacuna: namely, that the word *voyeur* appears to have no auditory equivalent?

Mastery and Metrics in Figaro

In May 1786, one year before the publication of Bentham's plans for an *Inspection-House*, the Viennese court opera staged the premiere of *The Marriage of Figaro*. But the opera became truly successful only after it was performed in Prague in December. Mozart, by the way, alluded to this success the following year in *Don Giovanni*, when Leporello, listening to the musicians play Figaro's famous aria (*Non più andrai*), exclaims: "I know this piece only too well."

Don Giovanni, as I have tried to show elsewhere, is a great opera about the ear: We listen to characters who themselves listen and, thereby, represent us other listeners on the stage and embody for us *types* of hearing.[25] This is also true for *The Marriage of Figaro*, where everyone regularly lends an ear. But unlike in *Don Giovanni*, which opposes to each other two attitudes of listening (the distracted Don Juan does not want to listen to the Commendatore and the law of his "structural" or total listening), we witness here an infinite series of variations on the same single situation: that of over-hearing.

In act 1, in the recitative of the fourth scene, Susanna and Marcellina listen to each other and secretly observe each other (Marcellina: "I'll pretend not to see her"; Susanna: "She is talking about me"). In the sixth scene, Cherubino hides behind a chair when the Count arrives and hears all of his words addressed to Susanna. In the seventh scene, not wanting to be seen by Basilio, this time it is the Count who hides behind the same chair, while Cherubino (who managed to jump unobserved to the other side of the chair) is covered by Susanna with a dress: This way there will be now *two* of them who overhear her conversation with Basilio. In the end, the Count emerges from his hiding place and reveals himself for a *terzetto*, at the conclusion of which he accidentally lifts the robe and discovers Cherubino. Hence the following exchange: "Count (to Susanna): 'My God! Then he heard everything I was saying to you!' Cherubino: 'I tried as hard as I could not to hear!'"

In short, in *The Marriage of Figaro*, everyone is spying on everyone else, thereby forming a network of receivers and auditory relays whose complexity defies analysis. The madness of this day ("la folle journée," according to the subtitle of Beaumarchais's play that inspired Mozart's librettist, Da Ponte) might be primarily the result of a general embroilment in overhearing. This is exactly where the political content of the opera is concentrated: in its ceaselessly varied exposure of listening as overhearing, which is to say, as a will to mastery.

Many have commented on the supposed tempering of the (pre)revolutionary content of Beaumarchais's play as it was adapted by Da Ponte for Mozart. In fact, the *Mémoires* of the Italian librettist have no doubt contributed to the belief in this attenuation in response to Joseph II's censorship, especially passages such as the following, which relates his conversation with the emperor:

> In conversation with me one day in this connection, [Mozart] asked me whether I could easily make an opera from a comedy by Beaumarchais—*Le Mariage de Figaro*. I liked the suggestion very much, and promised him to write one. But there was a very great difficulty to overcome. A few days previous, the Emperor had forbidden the company at the German theater to perform that comedy, which was too licentiously written, he though, for a self-respecting audience. How then propose it to him for an opera? . . . I set to work, accordingly, and as fast as I wrote the words, Mozart set them to music. In six weeks everything was in order. . . . Seizing that opportunity, I went, without saying a word to a living person, to offer *Figaro* to the Emperor:
> "What?" he said. . . . "This *Mariage de Figaro*—I have just forbidden the German troupe to use it!"
> "Yes, Sire," I rejoined, "but I was writing an opera, and not a comedy. I had to omit many scenes and to cut others quite considerably. I have omitted or cut anything that might offend good taste or public decency at a performance over which the Sovereign Majesty might preside."[26]

It is true that Da Ponte's version eliminates several of the scenes that were the most subversive in relation to the social order of the Ancien Régime. For instance, in the third scene of act 5, in which Napoleon later claimed to have heard "the whole Revolution," Figaro declares the following: "You think that because you are a great lord you are a great genius! Nobility, wealth, rank, high positions, such things make a man proud. But what did you ever do to earn them? Chose your parents carefully, that's all."[27] Even if such retorts did in fact disappear from the opera, the latter nevertheless does contain additions in relation to the theatrical piece, among which a *dance lesson* given by Figaro should not be underestimated when it comes to the reversal of values. This cavatina (act 1, scene 2) not only attributes to Figaro a speech that comes fairly close to being an insult to the Count, but above all it also employs a code of choreographic figures that, more so than words, destabilizes established hierarchies.

We listen to Figaro as he is alone in the nuptial chamber rearranging it. He appears to be dreaming of revenge against his master, whose intentions with Susanna are now known to him. The cavatina opens with the famous aria *Se vuol ballare*: "If you would dance, my pretty Count, / I'll play the tune on my little guitar. / If you will come to my dancing school / I'll gladly teach you the capriole." Figaro's words are accompanied here by the rhythm of a minuet: a dance of noble and ceremonial nature, that a thinker like Johann Georg Sulzer, in the same period, incidentally associated with "assemblages of persons who distinguish themselves by a fine manner of living."[28] But before too long the minuet turns into a contredanse that culminates with Figaro swearing to "turn all of [the Count's] schemes inside out" (*tutte le macchine rovescierò*).

Mozart is playing here in a consistent manner with, on the one hand, the code of court dances inherited from the baroque, such the minuet and, on the other hand, the contredanse, which, imported from England toward the end of the seventeenth century, occupied a singular position in the choreographic landscape before the French Revolution. Unlike the minuet, the contredanse does not have a fixed rhythmic structure. It subverts earlier customs by presenting itself as what we could call "a dance without dance," indifferent to the codes characteristic of the Ancien Régime.[29] The contredanse, which is practiced in *dance halls* rather than at the court or in salons, is not the typical expression of singular individuals: It is essentially a dance of *groups* that does not put the emphasis on the steps and movements linked to some coded affect but rather on the *figures* through which the couples are brought together and separated from each other in the midst of a large gathering.[30]

The *Encyclopédie méthodique*, published by Étienne Framéry in 1791, clearly recognized this revolutionary social dimension that contredanse ended up acquiring: In the entry devoted to it, Framéry derives its name from the English expression "country dance" and recalls that the number of participants is not fixed. As a result, he writes, this dance breaks with the "amour-propre" that motivated the old minuet, a dance performed theatrically by a couple for an audience, in order to express on the contrary "a sentiment of joy" that increases in proportion to the number of dancers and needs no audience at all.

These are the implications of the cavatina in which Figaro, in a sort of waking dream, leads his master from the dignified nobility of the minuet toward the excessive revolutionary contredanse of the masses.

But the subversive dimension of Mozartian writing does not limit itself to this generic manipulation of dance codes. Against the background of this choreographic feature, what carries the political resonances of the opera over to the tiniest details of its musical texture is the inscription of *mastery* into *measure* and *metrics*.

Thus, immediately after the overture, Figaro and Susanna's duettino (act 1, scene 1) stages a genuine operation of musical geometry. Figaro opens this first duet by singing *misurando* (according to the instructions of the score). Of course, it is his nuptial chamber that he surveys by measuring its space step by step, with movements of increasing amplitude. He counts: "Five . . . ten . . . twenty . . . thirty . . . thirty-six . . . forty-three," and the dimensions that he measures grow right in front of our eyes until they coincide with those of the room. While he is singing his measurements (*cinque, dieci, venti,* . . .), his vocal line, in the increasing intervals that it describes, transposes and literally follows the ascending progression of numbers. Listening to the opening of *The Marriage of Figaro*, we hear a sonorous space open up and delimit itself. It is this space that Figaro surveys and exposes step by step with his voice.

Based on this measurement, the musical plot begins to unfold with the recitative that follows. "What are you measuring, my dearest Figaro?," Susanna asks. And she peremptorily tells him that she won't stay in this room lent to them by the Count. In order to understand Susanna's mistrust, we have to first listen to the second duettino that follows almost immediately.

Figaro sings first. He insists that the location of the room, *situated between the Count and Countess's rooms*, is most practical: "If perchance Madame / should call you at night / ding ding: in two steps / from here you'd be there. / And then when the time comes / that my master wants me, / dong dong: in three bounds / I am ready to serve him." *Due passi, tre salti.* As we can see, this second duet is also introduced by reference to *steps* and *bounds* that cover a certain space. Musically, Figaro's vocal line is delimited in its amplitude by these *markers*, the sounds of the Countess's or the Count's bells (*ding ding, dong dong*, sung high and low, respectively). To put it differently, the same way that the rooms of the masters frame the servants' nuptial chamber, in this passage these bells provide the *frame* for Figaro's song, its lower and upper limits.

These are the same vocal markers that Susanna takes up in the next part of the duet in order to turn them into the frontiers of a musical space into which she can introduce her doubts: "Likewise some morning / the dear little Count, / ding ding: may send you / some three miles away, / ding, ding, dong dong: the devil may / send him to my door, / and behold, in three bounds . . ." In an admirable variation on Figaro's previous couplets (playing with a marvelous subtlety on the displacements and dissymmetries of sharp feminine bell sounds in relation to those of a masculine and grave threat), Susanna turns these physical as well as sonorous spaces into something uncertain and troubling: The proximity of a few steps could hide the distance of miles, and the comfortable bounds of the servant become the diabolical leaps of the master.

It is the following recitative that drives this point home: After having told Figaro to listen and keep quiet, Susanna informs him that the Count intends to take advantage of his "feudal right" with her in spite of the fact that he had already abolished this right. This threat that hovers over the servant couple is so much more imminent since their room is located between the rooms of the masters, exactly like their vocal space is circumscribed by the sounds of the bells that they must heed.

The space—both musical and theatrical—occupied by the servants is, thus, potentially a space of auditory telesurveillance. If they can easily hear the bells, then the masters can also hear, perceive, or overhear them.[31]

As we can see (or hear), Mozart appears to have displaced the political content of Beaumarchais's play *to the interior of the music.* As such, it is inside the auditory spaces of the work that musical *measure* recasts the relations of *mastery.*

Figaro, Susanna, the Count, the Countess, Cherubino. . . . All of them listen. All of them overhear. While listening to them, in my turn, I ask myself: What is the age of their ears, this age that appears to be simultaneously so close yet so distant from those of Bentham's inspectors?

Cherubino is a young page, while the Count appears to be an old rogue. But the age of the characters, as narrated to us by the libretto, is of little consequence. I would rather situate them, the bearers of these fictive ears that are nevertheless so present to mine, I would like to inscribe them into an archaeological stratigraphy, into a genealogy of listening beginning with what Nietzsche described as "the longest human age there has ever been," that of the fright of the hiding prey.[32]

The age of fear—the first age of listening, its long childhood. Its primitive stratum that, far from fading away, will be simply covered over by other subsequently deposited layers that can't prevent it from reemerging later. Thus, Nietzsche's claim that music is "an art of night and twilight" could be understood as saying that music retains something of this archaic fear despite the different stratifications that come between them.[33]

This fright, this primary terror should not be attributed to the passivity of the primitive ear as Adorno tended to believe.[34] To put it differently, it is not because the ear does not have lids that it is reduced to being merely a simple exposure, a pure panicky opening to everything that happens to it: This archaic listening, the archi-listening, if it exists, cannot be either a zero degree or a threat from which a more sophisticated listening would have to protect itself in order to be able to construct itself. To the contrary, it is even possible that fear is in a sense the very power of all listening worthy of the name inasmuch as it is already (at least potentially) over-hearing.

If Figaro, Susanna, and the others are distinguished listen-ers, if their ears embody in an exemplary fashion this hyper-bolic intensity of listening sustained and woven by the most extreme attention, it is exactly because the age of fear lives on or survives in them. Following Nietzsche, we could say that the extent of the development of their listening is measured by the degree of fear that dwells in them and haunts them.

Roland Barthes seems to share the same position in his 1976 essay titled "Listening." The text primarily presents itself as an attempt at otological dating that tries to establish distinc-tions among the different ears that succeeded each other throughout the ages: "Along the scale of living beings . . . and throughout human history, listening's object . . . varies or has varied. Therefore, simplifying to the extreme, we shall propose three types of listening."[35] The chronological char-acter of this typology is absolutely clear, even though a later type never annuls nor simply replaces an earlier form. We have to uncover here the stratification of successive forms of listening:

> According to the first, a living being orients its hearing . . .
> to certain *indices*; on this level nothing distinguishes ani-
> mal from man: the wolf listens for a (possible) noise of its
> prey, the hare for a (possible) noise of its hunter, the child
> and the lover for the approaching footsteps which might
> be the mother's or the beloved's. This first listening might
> be called an *alert*. The second is a *deciphering*; what the ear
> tries to intercept are certain *signs*. Here, no doubt, begins
> the human: I listen the way I read, i.e., according to certain
> codes.[36]

If Barthes's first listening is quite close to Nietzsche's age of fear, if it resembles an archaic overhearing ("alert" implies watchfulness), the second listening is a form of decryption. As far as the third kind is concerned ("whose approach is entirely modern," as Barthes writes, also adding that this "does not mean that it supplants the other two"), it seems to bring about a spiraling return to the origins, unless it is simply the breakthrough of the primitive stratum toward the secondary layer. Indeed, this third listening "does not aim at—or await—certain determined, classified signs":

> First of all, whereas for centuries listening could be defined as an intentional act of audition (to listen is to *want* to hear, in all conscience), today it is granted the power (and virtually the function) of playing over unknown spaces: . . . There is a disintegration of the Law which prescribes direct, unique listening; by definition, listening was *applied*; today we ask listening to *release*; we thereby return, but at another loop of the historical spiral to the conception of a *panic* listening.[37]

In three steps, in three movements, Barthes's otology, his discourse on the genealogy of the ear, comes to resemble a *spiral of fear*.

Following Barthes, I am thus tempted to think that the ears of Figaro, Susanna, and the others are also carried away by a helicoid movement in this stratified succession where the panic of the first listening turns and returns.

When Barthes speaks in the first place of grasping "the function of listening" by the notion of territory, when he suggests that it is simultaneously "defensive and predatory" because of its inscription into a "space of security," Figaro and Susanna are already present.[38] I find them with their ears devoted to the "capture of the fleeting index," to the "bewildered expectation of the irregular noise which will disturb our aural comfort, the security of the house."[39]

From this listening "on the alert," this archaic overhearing, Barthes's oto-archaeology moves to another kind "linked . . . to a hermeneutics" that aims to decode "what is obscure, blurred, or mute." This passage, evolution, or leap takes place through the invention of rhythm: "By rhythm . . . listening ceases to be a purely supervisory activity" in order to pose its object in the form of a "sign," in order to enter the symbolic order.[40] Figaro and Susanna, the Count and the Countess are themselves big children who, beyond the obsessive fear of their reciprocal surveillance, all represent themselves in their comings and goings, separation and closeness (*fort-da*) according to the codes of a rhythmical game: a dance or a choreography. It is through dancing their songs or by singing their dances that they measure or take measure of what they *signify* for each other. By becoming a minuet, a march, or a contredanse, the Count's walks, his steps, his movements cease to be simply threats of interruption and inscribe themselves into a system of signs that need to be interpreted and decrypted.

Finally, the characters of *Figaro* could be considered the contemporaries of the third age of the ear as it was described by Barthes (this "modern listening [that] no longer quite resembles what has here been called *listening to indices* and *listening to signs*"), at least to the degree that their roles, their positions as listeners tend to lose all their fixity.[41] Trying to describe what he believes to be possible to identify as a third kind of listening, Barthes writes: "There is no longer, on one side, someone who speaks, gives himself away, confesses, and, on the other, someone who listens, keeps silent, judges, and sanctions."[42] On the contrary, everyone listens and is listened to by turns and even at the same time.

Nevertheless, to draw the conclusion based on this that "a free listening" (that is to say, "a listening which circulates, which permutates, which disaggregates, by its mobility, the fixed network of the rules of speech") would announce itself here is not a step I am prepared to make.[43] Neither in the company of the protagonists of *Figaro*, nor anywhere else. Despite all the arduous work that Mozart performs to undermine the hierarchies of the Ancien Régime, there is nothing in *Figaro*'s treatment of listening that would authorize us to envision the coming of the age of this liberated intersubjectivity that Barthes seems to talk about.[44] There is nothing that would allow us to imagine the latter as anything but a naïve utopia. In order to grasp Figaro's, Susanna's, and the others' ears, Barthes's triple stratigraphy remains, without a doubt, insufficient. It remains so even if it manages to crack open the perspective of a listening that "compels the subject to renounce his 'inwardness,'" and in many ways opens up the path toward a deconstruction of the classic auditory apparatus.[45]

Perhaps we should turn here to what Deleuze, in one of his final texts, laconically identified as a possible extension of Foucault's analysis of surveillance.[46] Whereas Barthes seems to have postulated the horizon of an emancipation toward which the "dispersion" and the "shimmering" of listening disengaged from its traditional "modes" ("those of the believer, the disciple, and the patient") could or should converge,[47] Deleuze proposes to analyze the breakdown of the "sites of confinement" as a new regime of surveillance, as the transformation of "disciplinary societies" into "control societies":

> Foucault associated *disciplinary societies* with the eighteenth and nineteenth centuries; they reach their apogee at the beginning of the twentieth century. They operate by organizing major sites of confinement. . . . But Foucault also knew how short-lived this model was. . . . But discipline would in its turn begin to break down as new forces

moved slowly into place, then made rapid advances after the Second World War: we were no longer in disciplinary societies, we were leaving them behind. . . . *Control societies* are taking over from disciplinary societies.[48]

These "sites of confinement" or "interiors," as Deleuze enumerates them further on ("prisons, hospitals, factories, schools, the family"), form a list that recalls, on the one hand, Barthes's "old modes of listening" and, on the other hand, the fields of application that Bentham imagined for his panoptic and panacoustic project. With the "general breakdown" amid the "death throes" of these institutions, a web of new spaces opens up that Deleuze calls "controls": "Confinements are *molds*, different moldings, while controls are a *modulation*, like a self-transmuting molding continually changing from one moment to the next, or like a sieve whose mesh varies from one point to another."[49]

While the surveillance of disciplinary interiors implied the conformation of the individual as part of the masses in reference to a stable point or a center, controls operate through incessant and infinite adjustments between a web and what it captures. Perhaps a recent film provides the most compelling image of this situation: in *Enemy of the State* (directed by Tony Scott), we see as it were the mobile grid of the hunting net, the incessant transformation of the network that, through observation satellites, permanently maps the movements of the fugitive. It is as if the map adapted to every change of the territory.

Are we still talking about Figaro, Susanna, and the others? Perhaps. We'll see.

When Figaro's or Susanna's melodic line is temporarily framed by the sounds of the Count's or the Countess's virtual bells, isn't that as if they found themselves for a while in the field of a control monitor? Or even better: as if their singing movements were performed within the bandwidth of a microphone that, by capturing them, also determines their possible range? In the musical world of *Figaro*, the omnipresence of reciprocal overhearing appears to have as a consequence that, at every moment, reception (as a kind of recording *avant la lettre*) defines the possible registers of vocal movements.

But the frames of this microphonics, which weaves the musical texture according to bandwidths, displace themselves from one moment to another. They dislocate and readjust themselves following the flux and establish its positions that are, therefore, essentially *fluctuating*. This is why, beyond the plot and the theatrical apparatus that represent the *disciplinary* space of the nuptial chamber of the servants framed by those of the masters, musical space dissolves characters into a series of melodic or rhythmic parameters that reciprocally modulate each other and turns them into a flux of data articulated by instable relations of *control*.[50]

No doubt, it is time to forget Figaro, Susanna, and the others. To forget them, however, means to let them become music, to allow them to lose their traits and their individual silhouettes, and to dissolve them in the rhythmic or melodic texture of the flux that, carrying them, ceaselessly constitutes and destitutes them. What are they if not floating points or lines of flotation that compose, in the space of a few measures, a possible listening in the form of control or reciprocal overhearing? A listening at work in the work, a listening (in the primary sense of the French *écoute* as a "place from which one listens without being seen") inscribed in and prescribed by this architecture of notes, like a sort of bubble or an enclave in which the auditory equivalent of a *point of view* would stabilize and establish itself even if only for a brief moment.

* * *

These points or places that anticipate the listener that I am—that precede me and inscribe me in advance into the work when I overhear its characters who themselves listen—are to a certain degree similar to what the history of perspective construed as the place of the spectator or the position of the subject. Such an analogy, however, risks freezing the music into a tableau that presents itself according to stable lines of flight. How can we think, then, what we are tempted to call *points of listening*, if such things exist at all?[51] Following Bentham, should we conceive them based on the panoptic model of a *turning perspective*, a panoramic movement that could be that of a surveillance camera?[52] Or, rather, should we imagine them, following Deleuze, as a network or a web of perpetually modulated sensors with variable resolutions?

Telelistening and Telesurveillance

It appears that in the writings of the conductor Wilhelm Furtwängler we can see for the first time the outlines of what would become the dominant model for listening to classical music in the twentieth century: *structural listening*, to use Adorno's expression.[53]

This ideal, which also involves a practice of musical interpretation, is what Furtwängler calls, in a number of his texts, *Fernhören*. The latter is often translated as "distant hearing," although it would be more appropriate and more economical to translate it into French as *télécoute*, as "telelistening."

But what are we talking about?

Furtwängler explains himself in an essay on Bach that appeared in 1951:

> Here concentration on the moment linked with an unheard-of expansiveness is the immediate fulfillment of the moment

coupled with the truly sovereign view that encompasses the whole. With its alert feeling for what is close and far at the same time, with its unconstrained fulfillment of the here and now and a perpetual underground alert feeling [*unterirdisch-wachen Gefühl*] for the structure, the flow of the whole, with its "close experience" [*Nah-Erleben*] as well as its "distant hearing" [*Fernhören*], Bach's music offers us an example of biological and natural power like nothing else in music.[54]

To whom or to what does Furtwängler attribute this listening at a distance, this telelistening that he describes in terms of panoptic surveillance (as a "truly sovereign view that encompasses the whole")? To *music itself*, to Bach's music, since that is what the possessive construction of the last sentence obviously refers to ("with . . . *its* 'distant hearing,' Bach's music"). Hence, in the listening *of* music that is in question here, we must hear not only the objective but, and this is what really counts for me, also a subjective genitive: Even before being listened to by someone, even before becoming an object of an empirical listening, music itself listens and even listens to itself, according to *its* distant listening, this telelistening that would be *its own*.[55] Thus, discussing the listening *of* this music, Furtwängler is essentially saying that it is listened to at a distance and it telelistens to *itself*. This means that a kind of listening or overhearing must already be at play in it, even before some determinate listener would lend it an ear.

Furtwängler borrowed the idea or ideal of this *Fernhören*, which is opposed to the simple succession of musical moments the same way that the underground structure is opposed to the sonic surface (or like the totality is opposed to the detail), from the theoretical works of the musicologist Heinrich Schenker. He explicitly acknowledged this debt in an homage to Schenker written in 1947:

What Schenker places at the center of all his observations is the concept of *long-range hearing* [*Fernhören*] in music. . . . Long-range hearing, i.e. hearing applied over great spans to fundamental relationships that often spread across many pages, characterizes for Schenker great classical German music. This is the reason Schenker began again and again with this classical music, referred to it again and again, and never grew tired of demonstrating its organic superiority [*ihre organische Überlegenheit*] to what is considered music today. . . . In fact, the melodic, rhythmic, and harmonic elements of which music is ultimately composed are remarkably more simple in a Beethoven symphony than in a jazz composition. The decisive difference lies in only one thing: in jazz, *long-range hearing* is absent [*im Jazz fehlt das Fernhören*]. The intricacies exist for the moment in which they sound. The totality runs its course like a path through a dense jungle, where from right and left even new nuances, rhythms, creeping growths of all kinds approach us; then suddenly it is at an end and we simply step out of the jungle into the open again. In a Beethoven symphony, on the other hand, the first measure refers to the fifth, eighth, twentieth, thirtieth, even to measures up to the final cadence; and so it goes throughout the whole composition. The individual measure is simple, but the relationship among the measures, among the themes—the hundredfold correspondences and variations, intensifications and diminutions that are the result of this most ingenious *long-range hearing*—produces a mass of complications which, correctly comprehended, surpasses all that jazz has to offer, in the same way that a living organism, as a product of nature, infinitely surpasses every man-made machine in inner complexity. And herein lies the central point of Schenkerian perceptions: they are biological in nature and will make a place for themselves more and more as we learn to apply the perceptions of modern biology everywhere they must be applied, and that is, above all, in art.[56]

I considered it necessary to quote this text at length because it has a lot to say about what we could call a *politics of listening*. It is pointless, I believe, to point out the implications of what a reference to the biology of art could have had in 1947 (not to mention the metaphor of the "jungle" of jazz worthy of even worse discourses on "degenerate music").[57] What strikes me in this text that for the first time elevates telelistening to the level of a guiding concept (which, in many respects, Adorno merely paraphrased when he spoke about "structural listening") is that it blurs the distinction between Barthes's first and second forms of listening. Cultivated musical listening, which is in fact a deciphering of signs and codes, appears to be—as the example of the primitive jazz jungle shows—always on the point of plunging back into the age of fear: the primitive level of alert overhearing and the surveillance at a distance between the predator and the prey. And if the "great classical music" appears to be sheltered and protected from this fear, it is perhaps only to the degree that it internalizes the threat, to the degree that it turns the distance involved in listening into its *internal* affair. The fear masters itself in and by the organic panacoustics of telelistening.

Between the superficial details that I was supposed to capture from one moment to the other and the totality of the structure that I would have to survey (which means to keep an eye on it by having an eye for the whole), what place would this idea or vision of musical listening reserve for me? Where within the work does it situate or localize the listener that I am?

In the diary that he kept between the years 1927 and 1942, Furtwängler recorded the following few sentences: "*For the reproductive artist*: Every work carries *within it* its own 'distance,' from which one must consider it. To discover this distance and act accordingly is the principal duty of the performer."[58] If, mutatis mutandis, we were to replace the performer or player with the listener, this distance that Furtwängler speaks about would become, *for listening as well*, an internal affair: It is according to the distance prescribed by the work and inscribed in it, it is according to this internal distance that displaces the work from itself in itself that I am supposed to interpret, decrypt, or decode it (in short, to hear and understand it according to Barthes's second form of listening). Moreover, Furtwängler appears to say that this distance is one (he uses the singular form of the word) and measurable (the performer should find it). So much so that, without necessarily reducing it to a fixed point, following the example of visual perspective, Furtwängler nevertheless appears to postulate a line or a stable space for this displacement from which I can consider the work. Or even better: from which, in a sense, it considers itself, through me, by telelistening to itself at a distance from itself.

To put it differently, like Bentham's panoptic plans, the system of self-surveillance in the work seems to want to close in on itself: The one who listens and controls, like the one who watches and inspects, will find himself under surveillance by the structure of an apparatus that functions as a *closed circuit*. In other words, like the Panopticon that integrates all of its potential visitors into its own operations, the musical work according to Furtwängler appears to inscribe in advance, to catch and capture in advance in the grid of its web everything that happens and is to come, assigning it a place and a displacement that is immediately measured. This is why, in the end, according to Furtwängler's ideal of telelistening *the work overhears itself* in and through the place of the listener that it situates at the right distance.

However, this is not the case for jazz because, as Furtwängler suggests, it lacks the structure of telelistening. It lacks the notion of a work precisely in the sense of a closed apparatus or a closed circuit. Does this mean that in relation to the collective improvisation that constitutes jazz the listener that I am would no longer have an assignable place? That there would no longer be a stable position that I could (be made to) take up? To put it differently: What happens to my listening in jazz? What does it become in this primitive jungle where my ears find themselves assailed from all sides?

I am tempted to grant some relevance to Furtwängler's extended metaphors despite their ominous character during a time when the fascist and national socialist condemnations of jazz have barely been silenced.[59] In its unheard-of and unprecedented emergence, in its tracing of tracks and paths, improvisation resembles a hunt and the improvisator a hunter. As Julio Cortázar put it so nicely in a short story inspired by Charlie Parker, during improvisation the soloist pursued "what was trying to escape him while he was chasing it."[60] Hence, for the listener that I am, for me who follows and pursues the pursuer tracking its fugitive musical prey, does not listening to jazz resemble primitive overhearing, the perked-up ears on alert eagerly watching for the clues and traces that emerge in the course of the chase?[61] In short, it seems that there where the work and the horizon of its telelistening are absent (where the cohesive relations are missing that, inscribed in the *closure* of the work, would allow us to hear its structure independently from the jungle of details), there is no panoptic or panacoustic apparatus that could assign me a reassuring point of listening. As the one following it, to a certain degree, I myself am also dragged into the musical hunt played by the improviser.

It is, therefore, tempting to imagine that I am a kind of spy or secret voyeur. That I can hear the cries and calls of the hounds in their chase, which I can enjoy with a mixture of fear and impunity. A secret enjoyment that some musicians were capable of turning into the primary object of their art—like Robin Rimbaud, a British DJ, who, using a long-range radio receiver, hijacks, mixes, and remixes conversations that he captures in midair on cell phones. This artist, who chose for his pseudonym the name of his acoustic spying device (he signs his albums as *Scanner*), describes his own music as "voyeuristic" and describes it by deliberately using cinematic analogies: "I think that scanning sounds is similar to mapping a city. The opening scene of Robert Altman's *Short Cuts* gives us a quite correct representation of my work: the camera flies over the city and, as it covers the space, we hear people's conversations."[62]

The image of this mobile point from which the auditory map of what can be heard unfolds is quite seductive. Furthermore, it appears to lend itself especially well to giving an account of an ear attentive to the flood of an improvisation that ceaselessly composes and recomposes itself, like a scenery that unfolds for a bird's-eye view or like a territory that discloses itself only to the degree that one explores it.

But relying too much on this image would risk abusing the cinematographic analogy, since nothing whatsoever suggests that listening would organize itself around a *point of view*—even if it is mobile, even if it is in movement or in flight.

We have to ask if there is or if there could be, similarly to this point of view, something like a *point of listening*. This is the question that Michel Chion raises in his examination of representations of listening in cinema.[63] He shows that what is conventionally called "primary identification" does not exist for listening as it is carried over to the screen. This means that, even if the eyes of the spectator always adopt the point of view of the camera, this is not true for the ears of the listener:

> Even when the microphone is visible onscreen . . . , nothing especially makes us hear *through* that microphone. . . . Sometimes we even get a strangely contradictory effect between seeing the mic and hearing what we hear, which does not seem to be coming from that one visible source. This feeling is even clearer on set for TV, where . . . it's hard to accept that we are hearing "through" these little cylinders stuck on their lapels and sweaters.[64]

However, it does not follow from Chion's analysis that there is no such thing as a point of listening in cinema or elsewhere. Rather, contrary to the point of view, this point of listening is not structurally and stably inscribed in or given by the very apparatus of representation.

A Secret Conversation

Francis Ford Coppola masterfully staged the implications of this difference in his 1974 film, *The Conversation*, a great cinematic classic of surveillance that was shot in the context of the Watergate scandal.

The protagonist is Harry Caul (played by Gene Hackman), a private detective of sorts who specializes in auditory surveillance. In the epilogue of the film, after returning to his apartment, Harry begins to play his tenor saxophone. He improvises to a jazz record that he plays on his phonograph. In this way he adds his own part to that of the saxophone player who is already featured on the record. All of a sudden, as he is absorbed in this dreamy polylogue with these ghostly musicians, he receives a phone call. He turns down the volume on the record player, gets up, and picks up the phone: "Hello," he repeats twice, slowly with suspicion, but there is no response. We can hear only an indistinct noise at the other end of the line. Harry, visibly troubled, returns to his seat and begins to play along with the record that is still turning, as the camera lingers for a moment on the telephone. But in a few moments, Harry receives a second call. This time around, he lets it ring a bit longer before he picks it up again (meanwhile the record stops running). "Hello," he says, as we hear the sound of a tape rewinding. "Hello?" The voice of a man responds in a threatening tone: "We know that you know, Mr. Caul. For your own sake, do not get involved any further. We'll be listening to you." As if the threat had an immediate performative effect, Harry then hears a recording of his own improvisation that he had just played with the record.

Thus, Harry knows that from this moment on he himself—who spent his life listening to others—is being listened to. We, then, see him dismantle his apartment room by room, methodically and professionally, with a certain contented despair: He goes over everything with a fine-tooth comb, from the wallpaper to the flooring, board by board . . . But it is no use: Exhausted, not having found the microphone whose presence he suspected, Harry sits down wearily in the midst of the debris of his apartment and begins to play his saxophone.

Was it a coincidence that he could not find that cursed microphone? Is it possible that this experienced sleuth, this professional mole, was once in his life outsmarted and proven to be incompetent and incapable?

We have every reason to believe that the answer to this question is no, that it is not his fault at all, since the microphone remains for him *structurally* out of reach.

Why?

In a remarkable study devoted to surveillance in cinema, Thomas Levin has proposed a clever hypothesis to explain why Harry, despite all his efforts, could not under any circumstance find the device that surveyed him. The device remains impossible to find within the field of this scene, because it can be located in a displaced form in the movements of the camera itself:

> But it is right "there" in the film's final sequence, an extended high-angle shot, that slowly surveys the extent of the futile damage. Beginning in an empty corner, it pans slowly and methodically to the left until it captures the broken, saxophone-playing man, and then continues on past him until, having hit another corner, it suddenly and somewhat jerkily reverses itself and pans back, and then back again.[65]

The *form* of this shot, Levin concludes, its mechanical movement that consists of panoramic shots in opposing directions, plays the role of the surveillance device that Harry was desperately looking for. Its location is in another space, in another dimension, which is not that of the (diegetic) story but that of the technique of narration:

> But where "is" this thing located? It can't be "in" his apartment since the veteran expert would have long since discovered it: indeed Harry will never find the surveillant device because it resides in a space that is epistemologically unavailable to him within the diegesis: surveillance has become *the condition of the narration itself*. In other words,

the locus of surveillance has thus shifted, imperceptibly but decidedly, away from the space of the story, to the very condition of possibility of that story. Surveillance here has become the formal signature of the film's narration.[66]

Levin's analysis certainly illuminates the visual structure of this scene by situating it in a fascinating history of surveillance in cinema. Nevertheless, the fact remains that the spying device that motivates Harry's auto-perquisition in his own apartment is not a camera but a microphone. To put it differently, even if we consider that Harry is in fact filmed from the *point of view* of a surveillance camera (that he cannot by definition find because it is the very device that makes him exist as a character in the film), we have not yet said anything about the ungraspable and nonlocalizable nature of the *point of listening* that escapes him.

So I turn around, rewind the tape, and I replay the beginning of the scene.

When after his return home he begins to play his saxophone to relax, Harry does not yet know that he is under surveillance. He listens distractedly to the record that he uses as a background for his own improvisation, which adds a countersong to this recording. For the spectator as well as the listener, there is here what Michel Chion called "embedded listening."[67] Not unlike the operatic scenes that present to us, who listen to them, characters who are themselves listening.

But when a few moments later Harry hears through the telephone a recording of what he has just improvised over his record, when he therefore understands that he himself is being listened to, this shocking surprise at the end of the film freezes the blood in our veins; this horrible fall hurls the still reassuring and controllable figure of embedding into a truly bottomless abyss. The point is no longer simply that the musician spy finds himself spied upon. Harry now listens to himself on the telephone as having been recorded while he was himself listening to the record. He, therefore, is listening to himself as himself being part of this spectral space of phonography, this layered thickness in which he is now taken up and included. The realization that he is an object of listening is as if Harry were sinking and descending into the phonogram that accompanied him, as if his phrases from a moment ago had been swallowed up by the ghostly archive. Under the cover of the auditory surveillance whose object he has become, the listening *of* Harry (his listening but also mine, who is listening to him) appears to plunge or fall even further into the depths of sound.

So what happens here to the forms of listening that were hurled into this bottomless abyss?

Just like in *Figaro*, I find myself before a general embroilment in overhearing that I will try to describe as best as I can.

As I watch and listen to the film, I hear that Harry is being listened to as he is listening to the record that accompanies him. Or rather, I hear Harry who hears over the phone that he is being listened to, that he is being archived, as he is listening to the phonogram. Even before he begins to search the walls and the floor to find the possible microphone, he had been already expected, heard, spied upon by this watchful recording that now seems to swallow him up. But, along with Harry, I myself am swallowed by this descent into the abyss where sound appears to hollow itself out by *absorbing listening*: The same way that Harry is now included among the ghostly musicians of the record, I could also be listened to as I am listening to him, *seized* by this hidden auditory gramophony.

The result (a striking or, more precisely, a *seizing* effect) is a complete loss of anchoring. As if the distinction between surface and depth had become impossible to find, as if there were no longer a waterline for my ears. The masterly use of the soundtrack brings this out even further: While I see Harry sitting in the middle of the debris, as if through the lens of a surveillance camera, I hear the bifurcated or divided superimposition of his improvisations with the saxophone over one of the recurrent motifs of the film played on the piano. Nothing brings together, nothing harmonizes these two musical themes that, although simultaneous, remain strangers to each other, incommensurable, caught between an inside and an outside: between what Harry plays as a character *within* the story and the melody played on the piano that, in a certain sense, voices a narrative agency *outside* the story.

In the schism of this divided soundtrack, my listening trembles and loses its foothold: As I follow Harry simultaneously listening and being listened to, I am not seeing a substitute for myself, a representation that would consequently confirm my position of listening as a stable place. Contrary to what the movement of the camera shows, the *diegetic dissonance* of the two melodies (which do not *see eye to eye*) make me understand that "the place of the king" does not exist for me as a listener: My position is not a "truly sovereign view that encompasses the whole," as Furtwängler put it.[68] On the contrary, I am in an almost unbearable instable in-between—I vacillate.

This position that is, therefore, not one, that floats between an inside and outside rather than being *posed* somewhere, this place without place is similar to what becomes of Harry at the end of the film, namely a *double agent*. He works for and against the company that is employing him as a detective: He spies on its behalf; he records private conversations for them; but while doing all this, he discovers some criminal activities that he was not supposed to know about.[69] Similarly, in a certain sense my own listening is working *for* the subject that I am, the subject who sees and oversees and aims for a panacoustic mastery from the distance of an external sovereignty outside of the music or outside of the plot. But my listening also works with the characters that I follow precisely *against* this subject, since it exposes me to what surprises and destitutes me in my superior position in order to engulf me in sound.

In short, what *The Conversation* whispers to me is that, in relation to music or sound, there is no stable or stabilized point of listening fixed in a panacoustic edifice. There are only moving strata, only the sand in which we sink into the depths—even if it is true that the illusion of a Panacousticon is always ready to reemerge, as Furtwängler's telelistening shows. This is the *image* that is created when an alert listening is congealed into a "view that encompasses the whole." And the exclusion of jazz is one of its symptoms.

Underground Passage: The Mole in Its Burrow

Often, when I am all ears, on the alert, carefully lending an ear, I tell myself that *I am a listening*.[1] As if, while I am listening and give myself over to listening, I belonged to it: I am the listening that I am performing, and perhaps I am nothing but this listening, since my whole existence, every fiber of my being seems to converge in this single, unique, absorbing action or passion: opening my ears.

But this apparent gathering of myself in the most acute auditory attention should not conceal another possible figure for what I am when I am a listening, another figure that is more underground, more archaic, and more deeply burrowed. *A listener*, according to the archaic meaning of the French word *une écoute* that I managed to flush out in our old dictionaries, is a guard stationed in a mining tunnel charged with monitoring the progression, the development of the enemy miner's work.

Which is to say that when I am a listening, I am also and perhaps above all a mole.

Kafka's unfinished short story "The Burrow" gives voice to exactly such a mole.[2] Of course, there is nothing in Kafka's text that would allow us to determine precisely what kind of a mammal we are dealing with. But that is not the question at all. Rather than the exact zoological identity of the inhabitant of this underground labyrinth, what counts is its actions, as they are described all through the story. The narrator of "The Burrow" presents itself as someone who spends its whole life digging, like those excavating machines that are called "tunnel-boring machines" or, more precisely, "moles" in the drilling industry.

This soil animal, whatever it might be, does not only dig but also does not cease to listen, to prick up its ears to survey the security of its lair. Or, as the German title of the short story suggests, to ensure the integrity of its *Bau*, which also means: its construction, edifice, its building structures. . . . In short, in this marvelous little tale (which also could have been called "The Structure" or "The Work"), the animal is listening to all the noises that might announce a threat.[3] It is, also, a listening guard. In the building that is its own home, at the crossroads of the tunnels that it had opened, it is on the alert:

> Despite all my vigilance, may I not be attacked from some quite unexpected quarter? I live in peace in the inmost chamber of my house [*im Innersten meines Hauses*], and meanwhile the enemy may be burrowing his way slowly and stealthily straight toward me. . . . And it is not only by external enemies [*äußeren Feinde*] that I am threatened. There are also enemies in the bowels of the earth [*im Innern der Erde*]. . . . They come, you hear the scratching of their claws just under you in the ground, which is their element, and already you are lost. Here it is of no avail to console yourself with the thought that you are in your own house; far rather are you in theirs [*Hier gilt auch nicht, daß man in seinem Haus ist, vielmehr ist man in ihrem Haus*].[4]

Being at home, in the innermost chamber of its own house, the listener (the vigilant animal spirit that animates the work of art and watches over it) is also in the home of the other. The inside and the outside are blurred for this guard that I call a mole, that is to say, a spy who infiltrates, burrows into, and hides in the environment that it observes.

In this *topmology* of the burrow or underground construction (which also recalls the "underground alert feeling [*unterirdisch-wachen Gefühl*] for the structure" that Furtwängler discussed), what is missing is an external point of observation.[5] In order to supervise, to see if there is a threat or a danger, to *lucidly* evaluate the situation, the mole must exit its lair to gain access to and, thereby, also to expose itself to visible *light*:

> I then cautiously raise the trapdoor and slip outside, let it softly fall back again, and fly as fast as I can from the treacherous spot. . . . I seek out a good hiding place and keep watch [*belauere*] on the entrance of my house—this time from outside—for whole days and nights. Call it foolish if you like; it gives me infinite pleasure and reassures me. At such times it is as if I were not so much looking at my house as at myself sleeping, and had the joy of being in a profound slumber and simultaneously of keeping vigilant guard over myself [*mich scharf bewachen zu können*].[6]

Returning from these apotropaic excursions into the external element of the visible, the lookout becomes once again a listener. In the interior of this surveillance apparatus that is at the same time the structure of the burrows, everything passes through the ear. The underground mole, the figure for myopia and blindness if there ever was one, can no longer *see* its enemies or adversaries: "I have never seen them [*nie gesehen*], but legend tells of them and I firmly believe in them. They are creatures of the inner earth; not even legend can describe them. Their very victims can scarcely have seen them [*kaum gesehen*]."[7]

These burrows where rumor and hearsay reign, this underground building resembles the strange prison that Umberto Eco ironically described under the name *Anopticon*: Unlike Bentham's Panopticon, this construction (*Bau*) is organized in such a manner that the guard is the only one who is visible yet he himself cannot see.[8]

The burrow-structure is certainly anoptic, since there everything seems to radically escape the order of the visible.

Returning underground, coming back to its home, the mole first hears the surrounding silence: "But the most beautiful thing about my burrow is the stillness."[9] Of course, buried in the structure, the listening guard seems to expect the irruption that will disturb this calm. The silence is "deceptive" because "at any moment it may be shattered and then all will be over." The anxious mole, the guard, is sometimes alarmed: "I start up out of profound sleep and listen, listen into the stillness [*ich lausche, lausche in die Stille*] which reigns here unchanged day and night." But at first these starts do not last long, and this animal that we could call a *listening mole* (*taupe écoute*, similarly to what used to be called a *sœur escoute*, a "listening nun") returns to its sleep: "[I] smile contentedly, and then sink with loosened limbs into still profounder sleep."[10]

As long as there is no breach in the burrow, the listening guard (as the listening of and in the work) does not hear anything. It is a silent, dull, and drowsy listener. A *sleeper agent*, as it is said in the language of espionage, awaiting its activation.

But one fine day, in the night of the burrow, the scene of listening irremediably changes:

I must have slept for a long time. . . . [My sleep] must have been very light, for it was an almost inaudible whistling noise [*ein an sich kaum hörbares Zischen*] that wakened me. I recognized what it was immediately; the small fry, whom I had allowed far too much latitude [*viel zu wenig von mir beaufsichtigt*], had burrowed a new channel somewhere during my absence. . . . The air was caught there, and that produced the whistling noise [*das zischende Geräusch*]. . . . First, I shall have to listen at the walls of my passages [*genau horchend an den Wänder meines Ganges*] and locate the place of disturbance by experimental excavations, and only then will I be able to get rid of the noise.[11]

Just like Harry Caul in *The Conversation*, the listening guard of the burrows, buried in its home, glues its ears to the walls with the hope of finding not a microphone (or at least not for the time being) but a hole localizing the source of the sound. The mole, however, is gravely mistaken about the origins of the noise, which he comes to understand only little by little. First, he thinks: "This noise [*Geräusch*], however, is a comparatively innocent one; I did not hear it at all [*gar nicht gehört*] when I first arrived, although it must certainly have been there; I must first feel quite at home before I could hear it [*völlig heimisch werden, um es zu hören*]; it is, so to speak, audible only to the ear of the householder [*nur mit dem Ohr des Hausbesitzers hörbar*]."[12]

But what is heard only by these *internal* ears is also what, little by little, deprives them of their mastery in the heart of the home. Like Calvino's king, the "listening mole" is listening at home in the other's home, inside the outside. No matter how much it searches, digs, and excavates, it does not find anything. Just like Harry, it ends up destroying its own home in vain:

I start on my investigations [*Untersuchung*], but I can't find the right place to begin, and though I cut a few trenches I do it at random; naturally that has no effect, and the hard work of digging and the still harder work of filling the trenches up again and beating the earth firm is so much labor lost. I don't seem to be getting any nearer to the place where the noise is [*dem Ort des Geräusches*], it goes on always on the same thin note, with regular pauses, now a sort of whistling, but again like a kind of piping. . . . Nor is it growing louder; I recognize this when I listen in the middle of the passage instead of pressing my ear against the wall [*ohne direkt an der Wand zu horchen, mitten im Gang lausche*]. . . . But it is this very uniformity of the noise everywhere that disturbs me most.[13]

As it gets carried away, deconstructing and reconstructing the building where it lives,[14] the listening guard in a certain sense ends up listening to itself: it gives in to *oto-suggestion*. As a result of the intensification of the hypotheses that it constructs, this entombed hearing appears to metamorphose itself into mere imagination, into what the French call the "madwoman of the house."[15] It methodically constructs theories that are increasingly blinder and more erroneous.[16] As soon as it begins to build theoretical structures and constructions (like a phantom or phantasmatic *Bau* that functions as a double of the real burrow), it *multiplies* the objects of its listening, the source that it is desperately seeking:

There still remains the possibility that there are two noises, that up to now I have been listening at a good distance from the two centers, and that while its noise increases, when I draw near to one of them, the total result remains approximately the same for the ear in consequence of the lessening volume of sound from the other center. Already I have almost fancied sometimes, when I have listened carefully, that I could distinguish, if very indistinctly, differences of tone which support this new assumption.[17]

The spectral enemy that lays siege to the listener's theater of operations, the phantom that haunts the underground opera of this acoustic drama divides and splits itself as if it wanted to be everywhere at the same time. In this splitting that it appears to produce itself, *in the end (the) listening (guard) finds itself under auditory surveillance*, finds itself exposed to being heard, and it also admits it, although not without reluctance and denial:

> The more I reflect upon it the more improbable does it seem to me that the beast has even heard me; it is possible, though I can't imagine it, that it can have received news of me in some other way, but it has certainly never heard me. So long as I still knew nothing about it, it simply cannot have heard me, for at that time I kept very quiet, nothing could be more quiet than my return to the burrow; afterwards, when I dug the experimental trenches, perhaps it could have heard me, though my style of digging makes very little noise; but if it had heard me I must have noticed some sign of it, the beast must at least have stopped its work every now and then to listen. But all remained unchanged.

These are the final sentences of "The Burrow," this uncanny (*unheimlich*) tale.

So what do I discover when, like a mole, I am a listening guard? What awaits me when I am blindly engulfed in the vigilance of this underground structure?

A noise, a sound that tells me that I am also being listened to. I find there the signal of the sentinel that I have doubtless followed, tracked, and pursued even without knowing it: the listening of the other as it preceded me in the work, as it had already expected me.

If it were necessary to yield to the temptation to give it a face, a visible figure that we can recognize and name, I would say that this listening of the other, hiding there in the heterotopia that dwells at the very heart of the mole's abode, is what is called in English *a bug*.

A bug is primarily a small animal, a "little beast" (as the narrator of "The Burrow" puts it), some kind of an insect, and even a virus. In short, it is an animal so tiny that it cannot be localized. But in the language of espionage, surveillance, and wiretapping, a bug is also a hidden microphone that captures conversations. It could, therefore, be the name of this unfindable point of listening that the mole (like Harry) is searching for all the more feverishly since it senses that it is being listened to.

Drawn by this phantasmatic point, the listener panics: the mole gives in to fear, and the work of art turns out to be not the place of rest and harmony where the ear finds the calmness of harmony (*symphonia*) but, to the contrary, an uncontrollable network of permanent danger. Uncomfortable and even terribly alarming as this perspective might be, isn't this the life of the listener? Its always renewed eruption, maintained in and by its anxiety, its disquietude?

In the Footsteps of Orpheus

Trackers, with Hidden Noise

It is in broad daylight that they, in turn, prepare to track down the origin or the source of the noise that will lead them toward the one they are looking for, whom they do not even know yet.

They are *trackers*.[1]

I would like to follow them in their ancient hunt, whose story now I hold in my hands: These pages from which their subdued cries and barks resound as if from far away. The transmission has been quite bad for a long time now: In the papyrus of Sophocles' *The Trackers*, the mutilated passages are so numerous that despite the efforts of philologists to restore them the text reads like a truncated telegram.[2] Amid the cracklings of the line (which every now and then jumps abruptly), I hear these fragments:

> Let's go . . . your feet, your step . . . Courage! Courage! . . . Oh, oh! Yes, you . . . forward, the thief . . . through cunning . . . coming to the end . . . How, by what means these clandestine, nocturnal thefts, hastily . . . if by accident, I were to find it . . .[3]

Hello?

Yes, I am listening, but the reception is very bad.

It would appear that this is the chorus, yes, a chorus of satyrs that, following the commands of Silenus, who is their guide and chief, decided to pursue the thief responsible for stealing Apollo's cattle in order to earn the promised reward.[4]

A little later—and I do understand it better now—Silenus speaks of "track[ing] down the abductor, the predator, the thief."[5] Furthermore, where the Sophoclean signal is truly scrambled, I can still get a connection through another line: To the extent that I can corroborate the information of one text by another, the play takes up again the argument of the Homeric hymn to Hermes.

The mission, nevertheless, is not simple: How are we supposed to follow these trackers, who themselves follow the path of the thief, when so many different voices are mixed and confused here? Overhearing them from a distance, how would I know what they are saying?

There they are, for example, the pursuers, divided into two semichoruses. The trackers appear to have discovered a trail ("It looks as if we have them!"). They follow it as they encourage each other: "Make way, and . . . pay attention. . . . Listen if any internal noise reaches your ear," says the second semichorus according to the French transcription that I am using. But when I look at an English version (another tele-scription), I decipher the following words attributed to the first semichorus: "if you hear any sound from the cattle."[6]

In the confusion of the different accounts that reach me in the middle of this call center where I find myself, I can nevertheless still figure out that the trackers in the end reach the gates of Hermes' cave, where the one responsible for the theft is hiding. They hear an "incomprehensible sound," if we can believe my French informer, who transcribed the dialogue of the chorus in the following way: "*First semichorus*: I do not clearly hear their voices, but it is clear that these tracks, these footprints, belong to the cattle: We can be sure of that. *Second semichorus*: Hey! As Zeus is my witness, the tracks turn around and go backward: Look at them. What does this mean? Why in this direction? What went forward, now goes backward; these contrary traces blur into each other."[7]

The satyrs appear to be disoriented—and so am I. Did this thief manage to mislead the searchers who were tracking him? Switching over to the other line, the line of the Homeric hymn, I learn that Hermes made the cattle walk backward. But beyond this trick through which the villain managed to cover his tracks, despite the jammed signal, I understand that the trackers are literally dumbfounded by the sounds emanating from the cave to which they had been led by the footprints. This noise (*psophos*) "that no mortal has ever heard before," that is not "anybody's voice," stops and terrifies them.

"Why are you so scared, like children, *when you have not seen anything*," Silenus yells at them, putting on airs only to take to his heels himself when the sound from the cave is heard again. It is precisely *because they do not yet see anything* that the trackers are afraid. It is exactly this *secret noise*, whose source is still impossible to find and is hidden to the eyes, that terrifies them. In order for the hunt to come to a happy conclusion, however, it is enough for the courageous coryphaeus to raise some noise in order to make Cyllene, Hermes' nurse, come forth from the cave; questioning her, he succeeds in identifying the origins of the sound.[8] Even if the ending of Sophocles' text is lost, even if I will never have access to it on my teleprinters, I know that as soon as the source of the sound is named (which is Hermes, the thief, playing on the lyre that he has just invented), I do know that the trackers have completed their search.

The trackers, I tell myself, were in the end lucky: There was someone (Cyllene) who could answer for the origins of the mysterious sound. But what would have happened, had they found the gates of the cave closed? If they had been led in their search to a secret noise whose source had been definitively hidden or sealed?

With Hidden Noise—this is the title of a readymade that Marcel Duchamp created in 1916 with his friend Walter Arensberg. This is how he described it: "This Ready-made is a ball of twine between two squares of brass . . . and before I finished it, Arensberg put something inside the ball of twine, and never told me what it was, and I didn't want to know. It was a sort of secret, and it makes a noise, so we call this Ready-made with a secret noise, and listen to it. I will never know whether it is a diamond or a coin."[9]

In this strange music box, in this haphazardly constructed artificial miniature cave, sound appears to hide itself. At least, this is what the title suggests, since the adjective qualifies the noun it precedes: *With Hidden Noise*. Yet when Duchamp speaks about it, when he describes and outlines this secret without for that matter wanting to or being able to pin it down, it is no longer the noise that hides itself. It is "something": "a diamond or a coin," or some other object capable of producing sound. But can sound, as it is in itself, hide itself?

Through the metonymy that it contains ("something" noisy rather than noise itself), the readymade could very well hide a secret more abyssal than what a cursory first reading of its title might suggest: namely, that what withdraws itself here, what subtracts itself here is the very possibility that sound might be hidden, if it no longer has a hidden face.[10] To put it differently, the real secret of *With Hidden Noise* might be that sound does not know any withdrawal, hiding place, or crypt. That it keeps secret and conceals the secret itself.

This hypothesis that the readymade seems to formulate would therefore repeat a very old discourse that has been readymade for a long time and has not stopped reverberating since the fall of the walls of Jericho: a discourse on the powers of expansion of sound that are impossible to contain. Sound, it is said, cannot be held in check, limited, or mastered. Consequently, you cannot enclose a noise inside a box or in a cave, because either it gets out and leaks through to the outside where the trackers can always hear it, or it is itself devoured by silence and, regardless of whether some old scholars like it or not, it disappears forever.[11]

Duchamp's readymade appears to have inaugurated a series of art objects that implicitly or explicitly, secretly or openly, refer to it.[12] Robert Morris, for example, constructed in 1961 *The Box with the Sound of Its Own Making*:

> The box consists of six walnut pieces put together as a closed cube. I constructed the box with hand tools: hammer, saw, etc. It took me three hours. While I was working, I recorded with a tape player the noises of its construction. Before closing up the box, I installed in it a small loudspeaker. On one of its sides, I saved a little room so that a tape player can be hooked up to the loudspeaker. This way, we can replay the recorded sounds.[13]

Morris has therefore implanted in the very heart of the object the auditory trace of its history. As if to increase the effect of its presence or, at least, the stubborn self-presentation of the thing that contains and encloses itself. But what emerges from the hollow body constructed this way is the rustle of an inadequation or a disjointment. Beyond its solid appearance, closed and enclosed, as soon as it sounds and resounds, the object is ahead of itself. Or behind itself. It is still or already in the process of constructing itself as the object that it is. And this opening that damages its integrity, this dislocation, takes place exactly at the point of impossible articulation between its insistence on being and the sound of its becoming. What does not come together and, therefore, detaches Morris's box from itself is that this sound is from a different time than the now that heretofore maintained it.

In the end, these boxes, which intrigue us with what leaks out from their enclosures, very much resemble the cave of Hermes. Before them, a whole chorus of voices has been getting ready for a long time to collect themselves in order to take up once again this old refrain about the emergence of sound and its sensible excess. A choir of trackers outside the entrance of a cave, the threshold of a lair where the visible footsteps get blurred, all these voices prepare to say and repeat that it is the ear rather than vision that provides access to the trembling interiority of what is hidden. They pronounce that noise, or sound, or music discloses, denounces, and reveals.[14] But under the influence of this rumor that reaches us from the depths of time, nobody seems to imagine that in order to compare the audible and the visible in their respective potentialities for dissimulation, we would have to ask if, in broad daylight, *a sound can in fact hide another sound.*

Like Sophocles in *The Trackers*, Hitchcock has used sound in several of his films as a clue in an investigation or a pursuit. The most famous precursor in cinema was without a doubt Fritz Lang's *M* from 1931, where a blind beggar identifies the murderer thanks to the aria from *Peer Gynt* that he compulsively whistles in the presence of his young victims before he kills them. Hitchcock employed the same actor, Peter Lorre, in the first version of *The Man Who Knew Too Much* (1934). The following year, in 1935, he decided to use a whistled catchy tune as the key to the mystery of *The 39 Steps*.[15] In the later version of *The Man Who Knew Too Much* that Hitchcock directed in 1956, the acoustic Ariadne's thread that leads to the child hidden by his captors is a little song, "Whatever Will Be (Que sera, sera)," that was specifically written for the film by Jay Livingston and Ray Evans.

Hitchcock, like so many others, did not only manage to turn sound into a revealing signal of what is hidden from sight (a voice that puts the trackers on the right track), he also staged in a masterly way the phenomenon of *sound masking*. Thus, in one of his final films, *Topaz* (directed in 1969), the spy André Devereaux (Frederick Stafford) charges one of his contacts with infiltrating the Hotel Theresa in New York, where the Cuban delegation resides in the vicinity of the UN, in order to photograph some secret documents concerning Soviet missiles. Devereaux accompanies his agent to the hotel; he follows the agent with his eyes as the latter crosses the street; standing on the sidewalk across the street, he watches the agent enter the hotel, and he sees him through the windows of the lobby as he makes arrangements to go upstairs. But he does not hear anything: Without any visible obstacle, the noise of the street and the sound of traffic mask and cover the inaudible words on the lips of a character whom the camera nevertheless keeps in its frame.

Hitchcock turned this masked noise, hidden by another noise, *dissimulated in the register of sound itself*, into the motif of a fascinating suspenseful sequence in his remake of *The Man Who Knew Too Much*. The scene is well known: The gunshot aimed at the prime minister must be fired exactly at the moment when the cymbals of the symphonic orchestra playing at Royal Albert Hall are struck so that the crime remains unnoticed. Hitchcock alternates the shots: The hit man in his box, with his accomplice by his side, who is reading the score following it with her finger, measure by measure; the orchestra, the choir, the musicians, the conductor (Bernard Herrmann);[16] the smiling prime minister, leaning forward, enjoying the music; the cymbalist looking at his part made up of empty measures until the final clash of the cymbals (with the direction *sforzando*);[17] the brief dialogue between Ben McKenna (James Stewart) and his wife, Jo (Doris Day), that we cannot hear since their voices are already masked by the music; the revolver of the hit man, still hidden in the darkness behind the curtains of the box; the *crescendo* that runs through the pages of the conductor's score, inevitably leading to the anticipated clash of the cymbals; the cymbalist standing ready to execute his only action; finally and above all, the great cymbals that evoke two big ears framing the image.

We have seen and followed everything. The dense audiovisual montage even forces us to examine, as if under a microscope, every note of the cantata played by the orchestra. However, what disappeared in the process is the "phantom sound" of the gunshot.[18] The noise of the crime remains forever a *secret noise*.

But it is perhaps in *Torn Curtain* (1966) that Hitchcock truly shows us the matrix or, as it were, the minimal mathematics of masking within the movement of the chase itself. In the midst of the Cold War, the professor Michael Armstrong (Paul Newman), an atomic physicist who has become a double agent in the service of the American government, defects to the other side of the Iron Curtain by pretending to be a traitor. In East Berlin, as he is trying to contact Professor Lindt (Ludwig Donath) in order to steal an atomic formula from him, he attempts to lose the man who is shadowing him, a certain Gromek (Wolfgang Kieling), a security officer of the DDR. He enters a museum and hurries through the rooms where art objects are exposed to view without so much as glancing at them. He is desperately trying to lose [*depister*] his tail.

It is at this point that the soundtrack takes over—in a film whose title, while alluding to the Iron Curtain, does sound like a promise of a visual revelation. In the museum, in this place of the cult of vision, we cannot see Gromek. At the most, we merely see his approaching shadow for a moment. However, we hear the exaggeratedly amplified sounds of his footsteps echoing through the rooms. But Gromek's footsteps mix and blur together with Armstrong's. On the soundtrack or soundtrail [*piste sonore*], trailing and derailing derail each other [*pistage et dépistage se dépistent*].[19] And I, who follow them on the screen, hold my breath in order to listen to Armstrong listen to the footsteps of the one who is trailing him: In order to hear the steps, the professor stops. He must remain immobile (even at the risk of being caught) so that his own steps will not mask those of the other.

Watching this masterly *scene of lost steps*, I am now reminded of Orpheus and Eurydice, who also walk and follow each other.

The Mortal Ear, or Orpheus Turns Around

Here I am finally at the doorsteps of what is considered to be the first, the very first opera of Western history: Monteverdi's *L'Orfeo* (1607), based on Alessandro Striggio's libretto.[20]

I am preparing to enter, passing through the prologue, crossing this antechamber where Orpheus himself is waiting: I intend to follow him, to follow his steps that lead him to hell, to Tartarus, to follow the one who, by the power of his music or his song, crossed the frontier of all frontiers separating the living from the dead.

Like the trackers that Sophocles staged, I will track Orpheus. I will follow in his footsteps until we reach the source of a strange noise. Shadowing him, I will listen to him as he listens, keeps his ears open, and lends an ear. I will overhear him in the midst of the catastrophe that he is about to experience, when his song appears to become a kind of acoustic mask that frightens him and makes him turn around.

But through this threshold where I find myself in the prologue that makes me wait for Orpheus's arrival, music itself is the first to enter, music in person, music personified. As an allegory or a prosopopoeia, it is she, Music, who is approaching and singing, announced by an instrumental toccata and a solemn ritornello by the orchestra.

Music appears on the scene. What does she sing? What does she say?

Speaking of and for herself, she says that she comes to us, spectators and listeners of the opera, from a river: "From my beloved Permessus, I come to you." She descends to us or over us, she says, from a stream in Boeotia that the Greeks believed to be the dwelling place of the Muses. Alone and sovereign in this prologue, Music sings her own sovereignty. When she sounds and resounds, as she says of herself, when she flows and pours her heart out, even the rivers and streams must remain silent: "While I vary my songs, now happy, now sad, / even birds stop . . . / no sounding waves can be heard on these banks [*né s'oda in queste rive onda sonante*]."

As Music herself explains, under her authority, in the kingdom of her absolute power, a perfect silence reigns as it *must* reign around her sovereign song. So, even the stream to which she owes her mythical origin must fall silent, since at this point in the score, right after the word designating listening (*s'oda*), there is a remarkable emphatic pause, a resounding silence.

What is the nature of this pause? To what kingdom, to what empire or domain does it belong? Is it the mute yet still musical expression of an *absolute listening*, of a listening attuned to the sovereignty of the one who requires it? Is it a demand, a helpful illustration of what Music, in her absolute power, expects from her listeners? From this point where I stand, on this threshold of the prologue, it is difficult to say. I will wait and see.

It is still within the same prologue, in the midst of its flood of words and notes, that Music, surrounded by a respectful silence, utters these strange words: *mortal orecchia.* "I," she says, "singing with my golden lyre, I like to flatter the *mortal ear.*"

The expression can easily pass unnoticed. Furthermore, it is often translated as the "ear of mortals," which makes it even less remarkable. But for those who know and hear in advance certain resonances that are coming later in the opera, it is something like an internal prophecy within the work itself. In fact, what we could call *mortal listening* is the reason for Orpheus's later disobedience or indiscipline as he makes his way across hell, for the catastrophe, as well as for the irretrievable loss that follows from it. To put it differently, what Music appears to announce here discreetly, on the doorsteps of the drama that is to come, is this finite, weak, defective ear that causes Orpheus to *turn around* when, in the fourth act, he hears a noise. And, as I already know, this is how he ends up losing his Eurydice for the second time, before, in the fifth and final act, he is condemned to hear nothing but his own complaints and mournful lamentations as they return to him in the form of fragmented echoes.

This fine narrative thread, to which Music might be making a fleeting prophetic allusion here, this discreet but essential plot element will irrigate, as if through underground channels, several passages of the opera that I prepare to listen to one more time: "The mortal ear" is simultaneously the ear of the mortal being that we all are as well as the ear that carries death. I perceive here, I hear here the signs of an implicit discourse, perhaps of a secret, of something still unheard of that hides itself, buried in the plot of *L'Orfeo*. A tale of listening, in short, whose fabulous morale would pronounce, for those who know how to hear or to overhear it, that Orpheus's faulty and defective ear does not belong to or no longer belongs to the kingdom of Music and its absolute power. That it might even be what interrupts Music's flow or flood. That this mortal ear that carries a mortal listening emerges only where Music in one way or another *fails*.

Like a mildly perverted Earwicker in front of his telephonographic archive, the well-equipped listener or overhearer that I am can, jumping from one track to another, from one index or signal to another, directly go to the crime scenes in order to overhear without waiting the scene of Eurydice's second death; in order to tirelessly replay the recording of an incident that could very well be a murder caused by Orpheus's mortal ear (*mortal orecchia*).

So I move on to the fourth act: Why does Orpheus turn around, disobeying the command of Pluto's divine law? Why this lack of discipline?

This *revolution* within the opera (a revolution in the literal sense of a turning, an about-face, or a turnaround) occurs at the moment when Orpheus is overcome by doubts seemingly caused precisely by *the fact that he sings*. Right before disobeying, Orpheus sings a song that speaks of singing, a song about singing: "But while I sing, alas, who can assure me / that she follows me? [*Ma mentre io canto (ohimè) chi m'assicura / Ch'ella mi segua?*]" For Orpheus, who is in a sense on the verge of turning back on *singing* itself, it appears as if singing, that is to say, the exercise of his purest musical power, were suspicious, subject to caution and a source of doubt. So is it more than a mere coincidence that, a bit later, after an unexpected noise offstage,[21] Orpheus exclaims: "But what do I hear?" [*Ma che odo . . . ?*] His mortal ear, his defective and suspicious ear, is attracted by this unknown noise, so much so that it moves away from the absolute listening that Music demanded in the prologue with her sovereign song, like a contract between her and her mortal listeners. For a moment, Orpheus's listening, the listening of this demigod who incarnates and passes on the power of music to mortals (and even to the dead in their kingdom), for a fraction of a second at least, the ear of this fabulous musician appears to have *failed*.

We could even think, as Orpheus himself suggests in his suspicious song about singing, that it is precisely by singing, that it is *because of singing*, that he begins to undermine the sovereignty of the song, to weaken the autocratic confidence and self-affirmation that form its foundations. Although he does manage to retrieve Eurydice from death with the force of his musical powers, he nevertheless sings: "But *while I sing*, alas, who can assure me / that she is following me . . . ?" Even before the offstage noise positively interrupts the flow of the music and the attention that it demands, everything happens as if through Orpheus's song singing eroded itself by eroding its own absolute power.

Orpheus (who is walking) and Eurydice (who is following his footsteps toward the exit of hell) resemble here Hitchcock's spies: In order to hear if he is still being followed, Orpheus would have to stop the flow of his song. He would have to fall silent on the spot.

But Orpheus turns around and *sees* his beloved who begins to disappear. Barely assured of her presence through this turnaround in which listening turns into seeing, Orpheus immediately loses his Eurydice. He loses her for a second time, and the survivor dies again.

Orpheus's ear, the ear of the musician par excellence, is therefore mortal. Twice mortal: It is an ear that carries death, a criminal ear, the ear that kills Eurydice; and it is the ear of a finite being, a being delivered to its finitude and its failure, to its doubt that reaches even music itself. In short, an ear that is simultaneously curious and suspicious, that does not know in advance what is going to happen to it; an ear open to the surprise of the event, for example, of a noise understood as a sign confirming a threat. It is because it is intensely turned toward the arrival of what is to come; it is because it is carried away by the desire of *prelistening* and of *overhearing* at the same time that Orpheus's ear escapes music: Orpheus allows himself to be disturbed by what disturbs the absolute silence of listening. He allows himself to be distracted by a noise that he himself appears to have called forth or prepared by his own doubts, and he overturns the fabulous panacoustic power of the sovereign of this tale, Music herself, Music in person.

This unsound mortal ear without absolute assurance (*chi m'assicura?*) is, in a certain sense, the signature of the opera, the mark of its singularity in relation to its antique sources. In the tenth book of Ovid's *Metamorphoses*, as Orpheus and Eurydice are walking (Orpheus in front, Eurydice behind), they are surrounded by a silence undisturbed by any noise or any voice. And it is in the midst of this absolute calm that Orpheus turns around. At the same time, in the fourth book of Virgil's *Georgics* (which served as the primary source for Striggio's libretto), it is only after Orpheus turns around that we hear three times a loud sound from hell, which appears to be the echo or the roaring punctuation of a catastrophe that had already taken place. Monteverdi and Striggio, therefore, effectively reversed the order of the events by putting the noise before the turnaround as its cause. It is through this version or inversion that they make listening sound mortal, that is to say, exposed by its finitude to the unforeseeable.

Furthermore, the revolutionary motif of the turnaround, dramatically condensed in Orpheus's backward glance, is musically prepared and underlined by the dissemination of a number of inversions and involutions within the musical tissue of the opera. It is as if the ornamental volutions of the vocal and instrumental songs that turn around and return to themselves announced the coming of the catastrophe. In short, depending on whether we want to allow to resonate the Greek or the Latin roots of the expressions that designate reversal, we could say that we find *strophes* or *volutions* everywhere in the opera.[22]

But Orpheus's turnaround is not only something prefigured by these revolutions, by these diffuse volutes and volts that precede it in the opera. It itself also produces more durable resonances as it provokes remarkable echoes in the fifth act, when Orpheus bitterly laments the loss of his Eurydice.

This final act, which is the symmetrical counterpart of the first one, calls on the scene a second allegorical figure: not Music this time but Echo. These two figures are the only ones in the opera who escape the human versus divine opposition, so much so that Echo in fact appears to be a replica or a copy of Music, its damaged or ruined repetition. Echo seems to take the place of Music, substituting herself for the latter as its fragmented version. It is as if Echo were a finite reproduction, a mortal double of Music herself, deprived, divested, dispossessed of her sovereignty.

But what Echo actually does with Orpheus's laments, what she makes with his complaints is no longer fully musical. It is no longer certain that Echo's repetitions belong to the absolute rule of Music. This time, unlike the silence that punctuated the song of Music in the prologue (after the word *s'oda*, "can be heard"), the interruptions and the chasms that Echo opens up in Orpheus's song, far from constituting a form of silent absolute listening, are the outlines of another text that reinscribes the opera into another scene, into the suspension of a certain kind of interregnum: by changing the order of the letters, by repeating the musical sounds but reversing the written signs, Echo, as the defective double of Music corresponding to Orpheus's mortal ear, therefore represents the ultimate occurrence of the motif of turning that haunts the opera.[23]

It is this discreet and diffuse hidden discourse of *L'Orfeo,* this implicit discourse on listening that we can detect in the opera if we lend it an attentive ear. It should be noted, however, that in this "tale in music" (*favola in musica*), which appears to be praising the fabulous powers of music, its very sovereignty is nevertheless undermined in a way in order to allow for the emergence of the fragile contours of a listening that is everything but absolute. The fault or failure that haunts orphic listening inscribes itself here by means of this *double agent* that overhearing is. The latter is simultaneously beyond and below, more and less than the total or absolute listening demanded by Music herself in her sovereignty. It is on both sides, *on this side and on the far side*: On the one hand, it exaggerates, exacerbates, *exceeds* listening by a drive toward surveillance that unavoidably leads it in the direction of seeing, toward the audiovisual totality of a panacoustics doubled by a panoptics; on the other hand, because of the same drive, it also destines listening to lose itself in the infinite finitude of detail, which keeps it captive of its own will to absolute capture.

Orpheus's ear, therefore, marks the limit of overhearing, the extreme point where its own power inverts itself in order to expose it to the accident of what is coming.

On the Phone: Papageno at Mabuse's

Dead silence on the soundtrack except for the voice-over that speaks and narrates. "I couldn't hear my own footsteps. It was the walk of a dead man."—says Walter Neff (Fred MacMurray) in *Double Indemnity* (1944), shortly after having committed a murder with the help of the femme fatale played by Barbara Stanwyck.

This sordid tale is a classic film noir narrated in its entirety in the form of a flashback as the confession that Walter, an insurance broker, records for his colleague Barton Keyes (Edward G. Robinson). At the very beginning of the film, we see him wounded on his shoulder driving recklessly; he stops before the building where the company that employed him is located; he stumbles to the elevator; he crawls toward his office; he chooses a phonographic cylinder and places it in a dictaphone. The recording device is ready: The story—the film—can begin.

The inaudible footsteps, the about-face of the flashback: If I had to put into images *L'Orfeo*, if I had to shoot the film that I imagined so many times while listening to the opera, it would be very difficult for me to dismiss these fascinating sequences from *Double Indemnity*. I would like to imagine Orpheus as a murderer who no longer sees his own path on the cobblestones of the pavement, as he is already dictating to Echo, who records and repeats him, the crime that he is preparing to commit for love.

Is this what David Lynch and the writer Barry Gifford had in mind when they coauthored the screenplay of *Lost Highway* (1997)? Be that as it may, the fact remains that they could describe the film, which has superimposed itself over my memories of the opera, by saying that in it "*Orpheus and Eurydice Meet Double Indemnity.*"[24]

The fact that the protagonist of *Lost Highway*, a certain Fred Madison (Bill Pullman), happens to be a musician is, of course, not enough to make him into a contemporary Orpheus. His wife, the aptly named Renee (re-born), a reincarnation of the femme fatale played later in the film by the same actress (Patricia Arquette), is also not simply an updated metamorphosis of Eurydice who returns from the dead. Yet the orphic themes that have marked the long series of the different versions of the tale since Virgil to Cocteau and beyond, these motifs (the loss, the descent to hell, the resurrection foiled by the turnaround and the echo) appear to crystallize here, on the screen of *Lost Highway*, in the residual images that haunt our memories long after their disappearance.

It is as if Lynch had accelerated the speed of the legend, filming right from the credits the mad pursuit of an Orpheus launched at high speed onto the "highway to hell" to the sound of David Bowie's captivating song "I'm deranged." It is as if the journey toward the kingdom of the dead and the return from it became a savage road movie in the desert that does not lead anywhere.

These opening shots return several times in the film marking the disturbing reincarnations of the characters. But the frenzied movement that carries them toward their doubles crouching and laying low in the dark does not only borrow the path of the lost highway. It also passes through telephony and a whole series of *telephemes*: starting with the one that frames the narrative (Fred at the intercom at the beginning and the end of the film) until that other especially disturbing scene that puts the saxophone player in contact with the "Mystery Man" who appears simultaneously on both ends of the line.[25]

Like the mysterious video recordings sent to the protagonists with surveillance footage of their own home, these telephemes have something telepathic about them. If *Lost Highway* is also a film about surveillance, it appears to extend into the dimension of time the panoptics of panning cameras and the panacoustics of tapped telephones. To see everything and to hear everything essentially means here: to relive what already took place or perceive in advance what is coming from the future.

In a short note that now appears remarkably prescient, Walter Benjamin wrote:

> The more the police expand the habit of consulting mediums in difficult and important cases in order to pursue criminals, the more vital the defense against such procedures will become for the criminals. The question that could then arise for them would be precisely if there are measures that could prevent an action from entering the field of vision of a telepath and, if so, what those measures could be. Particularly if these measures should bear on the external execution of this action or on the intentions of the agent or on both.[26]

Although there are certainly cinematic examples of such telepaths in the service of the police (Spielberg's *Minority Report*, 2002) and counterespionage (De Palma's *The Fury*, 1978), *Lost Highway* in contrast inscribes itself in the same vein as Fritz Lang's *The Testament of Dr. Mabuse* (1933). On the one hand, the telepath here is in fact on the side of crime rather than of its prevention; on the other hand, telepathy is inextricably linked to telephony through a conjunction whose basic outlines are already visible in Freud.[27]

So what can we say about this telephonopathy in *Mabuse*?

The opening sequence after the credits shows Hofmeister, an agent who infiltrated the counterfeiters in order to spy on them for the police, hiding behind a crate, as the soundtrack plays the overpowering rhythmic noise of machines. Hofmeister (Karl Meixner) is discovered by the criminals: He starts to run; he is pursued and barely escapes death. As the flames of the explosion that did not succeed in killing him dissolve in a fade-out, we hear the voice of Inspector Lohmann (Otto Wernicke) speaking about the *Magic Fire Music*, the motif from Wagner's *The Valkyrie* that he just started whistling. Lohmann is getting dressed preparing to go to the opera: "Today will be the first time that I will arrive at the theater in time for the first act," he tells his assistant, Müller. But the phone at the police station begins to ring.

It is Hofmeister. The inspector tells him to go to hell and hangs up. But Hofmeister calls back. He begs Müller: "For heaven's sake, he must listen to me. Tell him that it is a question of life and death." When he finally has Lohmann on the phone, however, Hofmeister is so paralyzed by fear that he is incapable of speaking and he cannot tell him what he has discovered. He mumbles. He is terrorized. The lights go out in the room where he is calling from. He blindly fires his revolver, and begins to sing like a frightened child in the dark: *Gloria, Gloria* . . . Lohmann, confused and helpless, can do nothing but observe: "He's gone mad with fear."

Thus, the telepheme remains interrupted, suspended, awaiting its resolution. And it remains so until the very end, since Lohmann's attempt to anticipate the closure of this phone call that sets the whole film in motion also fails: Hofmeister, who is found and put under observation, is delirious, and he continues to replay the failed telepheme from the beginning ("Hello! Inspector Lohmann?" he keeps repeating with wild eyes in his cell). Despite Lohmann's stratagem (he makes his watch ring like a phone in order to try to restart and finish their conversation), Hofmeister relapses into his persecution mania and begins to hum his *Gloria* without being able to say anything about what he knows. "As soon as he feels observed [*beobachtet*], he begins to sing," comments the doctor. Lohmann gives up. The investigation founders.

It is only in the very last sequence of the film that Hofmeister manages to pronounce the name Mabuse. But this revelation no longer reveals anything: Lohmann has closed his investigation. We already know the identity of the criminal who, by way of a hypnosis that he can exert on and through the psychiatrist Baum at a distance (a *Fernhypnose*, which is a kind of thought transmission similar to telepathy), signals from afar the assassinations he plans out with great care. Thus, the final resolution of the telephonic dissonance that remains open all through the film occurs outside the plot, as it were, in an appendix or a coda.

It is with an ear trained on these telephemes—or as Adorno put it in a text that we will have to reread carefully, with an ear as "rapid, versatile, and shrewd, as the eyes of the regular viewer of detective films"—that I prepare to listen again to certain clues planted here and there in Mozart's *The Magic Flute*.[28] The latter is not only a kind of remake of Orpheus but also a great telephonic opera *avant la lettre* that stages what I have tried to call an *architelephonics at work in listening*.

Here I am, tracking and following Tamino, Pamina, and Papageno, who themselves follow each other. I hear them as they call, wait, and search for each other. And while I shadow them, I archive the inventory of their tracks, the traces of their footsteps, as well as my own fragmentary listening of their telephon-orphic phone calls.

I have collected at least three clues.

Here they are in the order that I encountered them on my track:

1. The fifteenth scene of the first act celebrates the magic power of the flute. Tamino, to whom the chorus has just announced that Pamina is alive but that she is kept prisoner in Sarastro's castle, picks up his flute in order to give thanks for the good news. Talking to his instrument like Orpheus

did to his lyre and attracting to himself the animals just like his mythical precursor, Tamino sings: "How powerful is your magic sound, / sweet flute, sweet flute who by your music / make even wild beasts feel joy. / Yet only Pamina, only Pamina stays away. / Pamina! Pamina! Listen, listen to me! / In vain, in vain! / Where? Where? Where? Ah, where shall I find you?" It is at this point, in the middle of this plea that is at the same time an injunction to listen (*höre, höre mich!*, a sort of insistent "hello!"), that Tamino's appeal receives from the distance a response in the form of an echo: The end of its ascending scale raised like a question mark is picked up by Papageno's panpipe. From a distance, he answers the phone and accepts the call.

Papageno finds Pamina in Sarastro's castle and saves her. The scene of the impending reunion of the three is twice interrupted by the distant echo of the flutes responding to each other. We first hear this echo through Tamino's ears or through his receiver, who then hurries in the direction of the sound singing: "Perhaps the sound will lead me to her!" In the following scene, as if through a shot reverse shot, we accompany Papageno and Pamina as they are symmetrically approaching each other with Tamino. This time, however, the echo between the two flutes is reversed: We first hear the panpipes of the bird-catcher and then we hear Tamino's response from a distance through Papageno's receiver. "Our friend Tamino can already hear us," he sings in the same voice together with Pamina. So the two quicken their steps, but they are unfortunately captured by Monostatos.

2. The solemn initiation process in the twenty-eighth scene of the second act is also placed under the double sign of movement and the orphic power of music. Furthermore, it is once again a flute solo that guides this initiation, despite the differences in tempo and style, with the same pointed

rhythm that opens and marks the process. Walking together like Orpheus and Eurydice, the finally reunited Pamina and Tamino brave the trials of water and fire. Hanging on to the fragile thread of the sound of the flute, their only point of reference and guide in the midst of the darkness that surrounds them, Pamina and Tamino find the path that leads them out of the infernal trials unharmed. They did not lose contact: Unlike their ancient predecessors, their line was not cut off.

3. Act 2, scene 29: Papageno enters, like a subaltern Orpheus, like a petty Orpheus who invites our sympathies through his mockery.

What is in the making, in accordance with the dramaturgical economy of this comic opera (*Singspiel*), is the final resolution of tensions with an eye to closure—to good form in due and proper form. To be more precise, it is Papageno's final union with his "better half" Papagena: After Tamino and Pamina's reunion, this is a necessary remainder that is expected at the end.

Here is, then, Papageno, who accompanies on his panpipe his calls to Papagena. But nothing and nobody responds: "Papagena! Papagena! Papagena! . . . In vain! Ah! She is lost!" After his lamentations that alternate with the powerless tunes of his instrument, Papageno is overcome with desperation and considers suicide: "I shall be the ornament of this tree / by hanging myself on it by the neck / because I have lost the will to live / Goodnight, gloomy world!" And yet the bon vivant Papageno hesitates to end his days on earth. Interrupting his final act, quite comically, he several times addresses some "pretty maidens" who could hold him back in extremis—but in vain: "Nobody hears me! Only silence," he sings as he is desperately waiting for a response. Then, for a last time, Papageno starts up his repeated musical call by counting to three ever more slowly (*Eins! Zwei! Drei!*). During the silences that articulate his countdown full of anticipation, we are also listening along with him. Just like he does, we also perk up our ears waiting for a response from afar, for some generous voice that would accept this final collect call, this ultimate phone call before he decides to kill himself for good.

But, as in any proper self-respecting *Singspiel*, everything ends well in *The Magic Flute*. Three young boys interrupt in unison Papageno's fatal action and remind him that he has in his possession a set of magic bells (*Glockenspiel*). It is with the sound of this flashy instrument that this poor spurious Orpheus finally manages to summon his Papagena.

And from here, the path, the *line* of orphism within *The Magic Flute*—that links and connects at a distance those scenes in which characters call and walk toward each other— this shattered and irregular line thickens as it manages to fill in the blanks that interrupt its route. In the rest of the same scene, the line of telephonic listening appears as a dotted line whose points get closer and closer to each other, earnestly promising to restore the continuity of a straight line at the moment when the final residual dramatic tension is resolved, namely, the dissymmetry between a still solitary Papageno and the already reunited Tamino-Pamina couple.

Papageno, thus, begins to play his bells and, when the chorus of the three boys tells him to look around him, he is finally stunned to discover his Papagena. We, then, hear the comic duo of the newly formed couple in which the first syllable of their names is repeated: *Pa, pa, pa, pa* . . .

Papageno and his other half move toward each other, syllable by syllable, step by step. Their steps quicken. Their syllables (*pa, pa*) respond to each other more and more quickly. This way they seem to cross one more time, quickly as if through a shortcut, within the same musical phrase presented in two voices, the episodes and motifs that have already taken place: (1) the distance over which Papageno and Tamino called each other on their flutes; (2) the solemn initiation process that appears here as if it were fast-forwarded; (3) and finally, Papageno's desperate calls resonating in the void.

The musical phrase that Papageno and Papagena form together—like a game of ping-pong in which the notes and syllables are being sent back and forth between the two sides— this phrase, at every step (*pa* also sounds like the French *pas*), is in the process of overcoming the distance that still separates them by a few steps. We can hear between the two voices, in their diaphony, a sequence of imitations that echo each other and come to fulfill the anticipation that has remained suspended since Papageno began to call in vain without obtaining a response. What is being prepared here is, therefore, the telephonic reunion of stuttering voices, their imminent connection before the approaching happy end.

This dramaturgical resolution, the bridging of this interphonic interval that brings these tele-locutors closer to each other step by step and syllable by syllable until they appear to each other in the end, turns *The Magic Flute*, well beyond its happy ending in the libretto, into a veritable *comedy of telelistening*. Once again, the latter should be taken in the double meaning of an objective and a subjective genitive. On the one hand, this telelistening is the *object* of representation. It is explicitly thematized and repeatedly staged when characters listen to each other from a distance. On the other hand, in the final analysis it is *our* telelistening of and within the opera that is the real *subject* of this comedy: It is this telelistening that, in the final successful reunion of Papageno and Papagena, knows the fictive happiness of an uninterrupted line. It is as if we could hear the pure sound of connection, when the voices no longer call each other since they are finally united. The dream of absolute tele-presence.

Tamino and Pamina on the one hand, Papageno and Papagena on the other: I imagine these orphic couples in a film having a phone conversation on a split screen, that is to say, with the screen divided in the middle showing, as it has been done innumerable times in cinema, the telelocutors on both sides of the division that vertically splits the image. I see them as parallel images simultaneously present on the left and then on the right as they call each other.

Cinema often makes a conversation visible through alternating shots and countershots as the camera films in turns the ones who are speaking. We could then understand the technique of the split screen, a classic figure of the telepheme on the screen, as an acceleration of this oscillation between the two points of view to the degree that they both remain simultaneously engraved in the image, co-present in the phone call. One more step and they would superimpose themselves on each other through a double exposure like Mabuse and Baum in Fritz Lang's *The Testament of Dr. Mabuse*: Papageno and Papagena in an alternating montage of their voices that gets faster and faster, in a kind of double hiccup that spirals out of control, end up forming a unique double sound image.

The festive split screen that is formed and abolished this way at the end of *The Magic Flute* represents the absolute enjoyment of telelistening: Furtwängler's ears—and the ears of all those who survey the underground structures of great Music—exult. In the pantelephonics of telelistening, where every auditory instant is supposedly permanently in communication with the others, Music represents the fantasy of a grand call center, of a hyper-operator who ensures all connections, constantly and everywhere keeping in radio contact with her agents. As if Orpheus and Eurydice, returning in the era of cell phones, were each walking with their phones, connected to the network of motifs and, therefore, to each other.

But we must abandon this fantasy. Because what is embedded in this telephonopathic desire that animates their mortal ears, what haunts this desire and is ready to reemerge at every turn is the breach in the network, the breaking of the thread, the moment when they hang up.

Hello?[29]

The Phantom of the Opera

The Phantom of the Opera, the novel that Gaston Leroux first published in a serialized format in 1910,[30] on a number of occasions explicitly presents itself as a new variation on the inexhaustible orphic story. Especially when Christine Daaé, the beautiful opera singer, relates the story of how she was kidnapped while she was singing on stage and then was taken through the cellars of the Paris Opera to the shores of an underground lake: "The souls of the dead as they reached the Styx never felt greater trepidation than I did! Charon himself was not more grim or silent than the black figure which ferried me in that boat."[31] Later Christine herself says that she became "one of the flock of Orpheus."[32] But beyond these deliberate allusions, it is through the staging of phonography as the *entombment of the voice* that the novel prolongs the story of the fabulous singer who descended underground to hell. In fact, a set of subterranean voices entombed in the "cellars of the Opera" were responsible for putting the investigator-narrator on the right track: "Actually I stumbled on their trail while looking for the remains of the Phantom of the Opera and would never have found them if it had not been for the amazingly serendipitous accident of the burial of those living voices!"[33] These buried voices that were brought to light showed the detective narrator the path. As for me, I would like to follow them and lend an ear to them everywhere they emerge in the novel and its film adaptations.

The Phantom of the Opera is above all a kind of ballet of voices. A choreography, a waltz, or a Witches' Sabbath in which it is impossible to distinguish the singular from the plural. The invisible voices of the phantom are everywhere and their ways appear to be inscrutable. As Madame Giry, the usher to the mysterious haunted box, puts it as early as chapter 5: "The voice, sir, *was sitting in the first chair of the front row on the right.*"[34] Later, in chapter 10, behind the scenes close to Christine's dressing room, Raoul is spying on his beloved and observes her in the act of listening:

> She seemed to be listening . . . Raoul listened too . . . Where was that strange noise, like a distant rhythm coming from? . . . A muffled humming seemed to emerge from the walls . . . It was as if the walls were singing! . . . The sound grew stronger, he could make out the words now . . . he distinctly heard a voice . . . a very beautiful, gentle, captivating voice. . . . it came nearer, nearer . . . it passed through the wall . . . it entered . . . and then *the voice was in the room*, singing for Christine! She got to her feet and spoke to the voice as if she was speaking to a person standing next to her.[35]

We can almost hear in this passage, which resembles a belated version of the story of the walls of Jericho, through the suspension points that excessively punctuate the sentences of the detective narrator, through these dotted lines, the circulation of the voice that inhabits these tunnels and walls. For this voice resides precisely where the ears of so many moles are hiding in wait, from the spies of the Bible or Sun Tzu to the bugs that record Harry.

So is the voice that we can hear everywhere in the novel one voice or several voices? The key to the mystery, to this panphonics that repeats and echoes the panacoustics of over-hearing, is the phantom's ventriloquism through which he desperately tries to seduce Christine one last time: "I am the greatest ventriloquist alive!"—he tells her as she is trying to escape from him—"Perhaps you don't believe me! . . . Listen!"[36] And he directs or implants his voice at will here or there, in a general stereophony that defies space: "Listen to my voice . . . where do you want me to throw it? Into your right ear? . . . or your left ear? . . . Do you want it to come from far away? . . . or from close to you? . . . My voice can go anywhere! . . . everywhere! . . . and now, abracadabra, it's in La Carlotta's throat, deep inside her golden throat, La Carlotta's throat of tintinnabulating crystal."[37]

Carlotta—yes, the poor Carlotta, Christine's unfortunate competitor on the stage of the Opera—will be the first experiment for the phantom's powerful vocolocomotion. The latter, however, has warned and threatened. He had done everything so that she would give up singing the part of Marguerite in Gounod's *Faust* and leave the role to Christine. But Carlotta did not want to listen, and Christine found herself in a minor role wearing male clothes.

To better understand the significance of the reprisals that the phantom has consequently decided to exact, we have to imagine the scene as a whole. As the two rivals are singing and the specter is preparing to strike, hiding no one knows where, the audience is also divided into two opposing factions. On the one side, we find "La Carlotta's partisans," while on the other the presumed artisans of a proclaimed "cabal" preparing an "ovation" that was supposed to serve the other party, namely that of Christine.[38] It is, therefore, in a (theater organized like a battlefield with its antagonistic armies of applauding claqueurs that the phantom is preparing to intervene.[39] In this tense atmosphere, overheated as if in a combat, Carlotta's every entry and exit is greeted with a "tremendous reception," all of her arias with "thunderous applause."[40] Christine, in contrast, is met by the silence of the audience. In this war of listening, in the tactics of this auditory marking that the claque is, it is up to the phantom to reverse the relations of the present forces by leaving Carlotta and her troops definitively defeated.

This is what happens next.

Right in the middle of the third act of *Faust*, in the love duet, Carlotta is in the process of singing: "Oh, silence! Oh, happiness! Unspeakable mystery! / Intoxicating tranquility! / I listen! . . . And I understand this lonely voice / that sings in my heart!"[41] She is singing that she is singing, and she is singing that she is listening. She does not appear to be concerned, like Orpheus was, that while she is singing, she might not be able to hear, that her song could be a phonic mask shielding her eardrums. She sings, in all quietude and beatitude, that she is listening while she is singing.

It is precisely at this moment that the ventriloquist phantom begins to act. All of a sudden, a "toad," an "awful *skaark*," slips out of Carlotta's mouth:

A disgusting, hideous, scaly, poisonous, slimy, clammy, croaking toad! How had it gotten there? How could it have squatted on her tongue? Back legs braced under it ready to jump higher and further, it had crouched furtively in her larynx and leaped out with a loud *skaaark*! . . . La Carlotta could not believe her throat or ears. . . . It wasn't natural. There had to be some kind of bewitchery behind it.[42]

Encouraged by her partner in the amorous duo, the baffled Carlotta nevertheless attempts to start her aria again where this accident interrupted it. She begins to sing, hesitantly, moving step by step, syllable by syllable, but all in vain: "La Carlotta's lone voice rang through the huge auditorium. 'I listen! . . .'—The theatre also listens. '. . . And I understand this solitary voice (skaaark!) Skaaark! . . . who sings in my . . . skaaark!' [. . .] The toad had begun exactly where it had left off. There was uproar in the theatre."[43]

On rare occasions, the Paris Opera had no doubt known similarly intense moments of listening. On rare occasions, the ears in the audience as well as the ears on the stage have been strained in a fascinating face-off, awaiting the call coming from an unknown place to ventriloquize the most intimate heart of the telephone cord that unites the shot reverse shot of the singer and her audience. Like a parasitic call, like a phone call usurping the line of another, the phantom has marked more than once the scene of listening. He punctuated this division of alert ears on both sides, *between* the listeners who are all ears and Carlotta who sings the song of the voice and of listening.

The phantom's resounding punctuations are Trojan horses in the voice of the other, phonic bombs that can fall anywhere on this battlefield, in the middle of this polemology of listening that is the claque. As a kind of counterforce for a counterattack, the phantom, just like Carlotta's claqueurs but against them, marks the music by these ventriloquized croaks and clacks. He punctuates the music with repeated calls through dotted phone lines [*coups de points*] (in the form of those suspension points that Leroux overuses in his narration).[44] He disfigures it in order to engrave his signature. As a revenge, he inscribes in the fickle voice a kind of durable and memorable phonogroove that will be remembered for a long time.[45]

This whole strange case of ventriloquism and telephonic presence through suspension points and dotted phone lines [*coups de points*] in the throat of the other all began with the discovery of the recorded voices, encrypted and entombed as if in a burrow, in the cellars of the Opera. In fact, it is by way of a certain underground phonography, by way of the underside of the stage that the phantom, a puppeteer or projectionist of the voice, composes and organizes phonic space.

The sovereign phantom's cryptogramophony, the fantasy of a subterranean specter with just as much panphonic as panoptic and panacoustic power, evokes the ghost of *Hamlet*, who cries from below the stage, or Mabuse, who through his arborescent telephonic prostheses (the psychiatrist Baum, himself extended by his gramophone horn behind the curtain), reaches deep into the cellars where the criminals gather. A hyperbole of power, the enjoyment of unlimited mastery by the one who reigns, *from below*, over mouths and ears and throats.

It is this absolute phantom or absolute fantasy, *absolutely sovereign because subterranean*, that Brian De Palma was the first one, unlike so many others who also adapted it to the screen, to undermine or deconstruct with his *Phantom of the Paradise* (1974).

The phantom, as could be expected, has known a long afterlife and had countless reappearances in cinema since Gaston Leroux. Its first film version was produced in 1925 by Rupert Julian and Edward Sedgwick. The specter, played by the unforgettable Lon Chaney, who remained masked almost until the very end, is here watched by the police: In a document presented to the director of the Opera, he is identified as an insane criminal who goes by the name Erik and is described as a "self educated musician and master of Black Art" who escaped from his forced exile to Devil's Island and is "now at large." It is he who, after having charmed her with his voice behind the scenes, drags the beautiful Christine (Mary Philbin) off into the tunnels below the Opera where he lives. Yielding to his prisoner's appeals, he agrees to let her go, but he makes her promise that she would never try to see her fiancé again. But Christine does not keep her word: She meets Raoul (Norman Kerry) on the roof of the Opera in a memorable scene as the phantom, wearing a skull mask for the annual ball, spies on the lovers and overhears them. "Are we alone, Raoul?"—Christine asks anxiously—"Can anyone overhear what we say?" A quick shot responds, unknown to Christine, showing the cape of the phantom floating in the wind over Apollo's statue that towers over the frightened couple.

After this first reincarnation on the screen, the phantom has continued to haunt the set that was built specifically for him in Hollywood in 1924. Known as the "phantom stage," Stage 28 of Universal Studios is a faithful reproduction of the Paris Opera that withstood the test of time. Hitchcock shot there the final ballet scene for *Torn Curtain* in 1965. And Arthur Lubin filmed there in 1943 his adaptation of Leroux's novel, *Phantom of the Opera*, in which the specter is a poor violinist laid off from the orchestra who is also cheated out of his work: Trying to publish with Pleyel the concerto that he wrote, the famous editor treats him with contempt and refuses to return to him his manuscript. When he hears that his music is being played by Liszt himself in the elegant salon of the publisher, he loses his temper and, as he is in the middle of strangling Pleyel, he gets a tray of etching acid thrown into his face that permanently disfigures him.

Inspired by this last detail, Brian De Palma has shot a different scene in a different set. "My next project," he announced in 1973, is "a horror/rock musical which will hopefully combine the genres of horror and rock in one Faustian fantasmagoria."[46]

But most important, *Phantom of the Paradise* gives us an even more blemished image of the phantom's sovereignty than Lubin's version. Shaken and weakened, the specter is a poor composer, Winslow Leach (William Finley), who is expropriated, whose music, a rock cantata titled *Faust*, is stolen by a diabolic producer called Swan (Paul Williams). From then on, the musician in search of justice and reparations does everything to recuperate and defend his work. He even begins to haunt the production of the show based on his stolen score that is being put on in Paradise, the theater that Swan bought.

In the course of his enterprise of reappropriation, Leach is marked in his flesh with the stigmata of auditory reproduction: Attempting to break into the premises of Death Records, Swan's record company, he is crushed by a vinyl record press that cuts hideous grooves into his cheek as his face is branded by the mold. It is after this accident that, reported missing, he becomes a phantom without a face, hiding behind a mask the gramophonic scarifications that disfigured him. Thus, with his only remaining eye, Leach evokes a monstrous cycloptic camera, whose mouth produces only an almost inaudible voice, since the speech organs of the poor musician were also damaged in the phonogrammatic accident. In order to be able to enter into a contract with this specter without a face or speech, Swan first gives him a synthetic voice, by amplifying and filtering his murmur through connecting him to the devices of a recording studio.

From this moment on, Winslow Leach becomes a spectral and prosthetic being: a haunting apparition equipped with a prosthetic device who begins to exist like an animated copy. De Palma, in short, shows on the screen the making of a cinematographic character as a phantom whose life and voice have been artificially restored, as an incarnated audiovisual montage.

And this spectral being does not remain in one place. Like Leroux's phantom, Winslow Leach is everywhere: He escapes from the studio where he was walled in; he circulates behind the scenes, appearing sometimes stage left, sometimes stage right, sometimes perching up among the machinery and the scenery. In the scene that precedes the grand ballet finale, we find him staring at control monitors, the many surveillance screens of *Paradise*: Gaining access to panoptic vision—seeing both the killer hired to assassinate the beautiful Phoenix (Jessica Harper) and the latter as she is preparing to go on stage— Leach becomes a kind of omniscient gaze and dethrones in this role the sovereign Swan, who until now held this privilege alone.

Phantom of the Paradise could then be understood as the staging of a life-and-death struggle with an eye on domination by vision and a panoptic sovereignty that is at the same time a merciless war for the possession of music and the voice. The cruelest scene in this regard is the one in which the phantom, in the middle of a thunderstorm, out in the pouring rain surrounded by lightning, observes Swan making love to Phoenix. The reproductive producer takes hold of the body of this new star that he created, this singer who owes him everything. And the leering phantom is on the roof ogling the lovers through the skylight with his masked Cyclops eye. But Swan, relishing his power over Phoenix, appears to increase his pleasure by watching on a control monitor connected to a camera installed on the roof of his mansion the poor Winslow Leach condemned to witness his double dispossession: He has lost both his music and Phoenix, the one whose voice he loved so much that he believed her to be the only one capable of singing his cantata.

Watching these images soaked in the deluge of water, our eyes begin to tear up as we see the phantom, filled with sadness and resignation, close his only eyelid behind the mask. And we tremble seeing Swan's power, who enjoys seeing that he is being watched, while Phoenix's vibrant and deeply moving voice echoes in the background. She is not singing on the screen (she yields silently to Swan's enjoyment), but her poignant song, "Old Souls," that she has earlier performed on stage in front of an admiring crowd, returns on the soundtrack in order to accompany in a split screen the images of Leach's misery. The screen divides itself. To the right, Swan's diabolical smile appears amid the caresses that Phoenix lavishes on him. To the left, the surveillance monitor next to the bed shows the phantom perching up above while a tape recorder is running as it if were playing the melancholy ballad of the old souls.

At the end of this disturbing scene, Leach tries to commit suicide with a dagger. But even the peace of death is denied to him, since his life is tied to Swan's life by an infernal contract written in blood. The phantom's impossible suicide, therefore, appears to be provoked not only by his despair at losing Phoenix but also and above all by the fact that he can see the *mise an abyme* of the audiovisual montage of which he is himself the object. He, who already owes his survival to this phonic device with which Swan gave him once again an audible voice, now sees himself filmed and surveyed by the same Swan while the song on the soundtrack puts his loss on display in Phoenix's voice: "We are old souls in a new life baby . . ."

Surveillance, in the form of this film within the film, becomes here an abyssal eternal return. Leach, the phantom musician, the revenant, who very much wanted to die, seems to be condemned to relive in an endless loop, like a spinning wheel, the same closed circuit of his own mournful images. "And still return," Phoenix goes on singing.

If *Phantom of the Paradise* is, thus, a film about surveillance as the return of the revenant, it is at the same time the theater for a war of signatures—a trench war or, rather, a war of phonogrammatic grooves, inscriptions, incisions. A war of the deposited, imprinted, engraved, recorded mark. That is to say, also a conflict of punctuations, scansions, articulations, and points of editing: Who will have the final cut, the last clap or the definitive claque, on the sound or the image, on the face or the voice of the other?

Like the claqueurs of the Paris Opera with their "paid applause" (as Berlioz described them), the different mechanical reincarnations of this institution are apparatuses for marking the image and the sound: The English term for the claque or applause is *to clap*, and this verb also names a traditional form of indexation, since the "clapper" or the "clapperboard" is the small board on which every take of every scene of a film is numbered (the clapperboard is equipped with a "clapstick" that, operated by the so-called "clapper loader," signals with its sound the beginning of every shot). In short, the isolated clack of the clapperboard, the repeated claps in unison of the clappers who are the claqueurs, as well as the croaking that the phantom projects into Carlotta's throat are all (depending on the individual case, mechanical, manual, or spectral) forms of punctuation of the image and the sound. They are marks that allow us to survey the scenes, to find them by following their traces.

The visual clap appears as a simple fleeting interruption of the moving image, which can subsequently continue to roll without necessarily disturbing the stability of the *point of view*, a little bit like the blinking of an eyelid that does not displace for all that the perspective of the gaze. But unlike this wink of the eye through which the click of the clapperboard marks the visual take, the phonic clap is itself the *point of listening* that it inscribes every time. This is why, at the moment of its imprinting, in this moment of punctuation when marking blurs with masking, the phonic signature, this phonogrooving or phonography, is always a phonodrama, be it big or small.

Professor Armstrong in Hitchcock's *Torn Curtain* had to stop in order to hear the steps of the other who followed him. Orpheus, walking in front of Eurydice, already wondered: "But while I sing, alas, who can assure me / that she follows me?" And he had every reason on earth to be worried and to mistrust his tune, since (contrary to what Carlotta-Marguerite gave voice to in *Faust*) while he was singing he could not hear either Eurydice's steps behind him or even his own song. In order for him to hear something (and for me and for us along with him), it was necessary for a puncture point [*coup de point*] to intervene behind the scenes, this punctuation that produces marks from which listening can be born in the echo of gramophony.

The points of listening, these puncture points [*coups de points*] that punctuate and mark while masking, are always deaf [*sourds*] points: *punctum surdum* in the manner of the *punctum caecum* located at the center of the retina.[47] The deafness of listening, however, does not reside in the organ but rather ceaselessly inscribes itself directly in its object as it repeatedly stamps and imprints itself in sound. The otographic interruption, without which there would be no listening, is always deafening when it ventriloquizes music or the song in order to leave behind in them its traces, its repeated marks.[48]

If there is no single point of listening that would be stable, centered, and sovereign, and could maintain itself like a point of view; if there are only multiple target points or rather points of impact, like neuralgic or strategic points, it is because auditory scansion proceeds by several punctuations. The markings that the phantom listener performs, forever carried away by the flux without a reference point or a contact point, resemble exclamation points or question marks for which the claque or the croak in the throat of the other are merely the most indiscreet examples. In short, whether they represent organized clapping or spectrographic indexation, these auditory interruptions are something like punches that stamp the soundtrack by piercing it or riddling it with holes. Sometimes the latter can become the soundtrack of a whole life, like Serge Gainsbourg's endless "little holes" in his unforgettable song "Le Poinçonneur des Lilas" (The Ticket Puncher of Lilas).[49]

This otographic signature is quite simply the condition of the appropriation without which listening would not be possible. The claqueurs of the Paris Opera merely marked their listening, inscribed it directly into the music that they had signed. And moving from the Opera to the rock palace, in the story of "exappropriation" that *Phantom of the Paradise* stages, we witness a sort of overview of the different forms of marking music.[50]

Disappointed by the Beach Bums' violation of his *Faust* cantata arranged in the style of surf music, De Palma's phantom places a time bomb in the trunk of the convertible that is pushed on the stage. The ominous tick-tock that we can hear all through this scene shown on a split screen could be understood as a sonic dotted line, a phonic punctuation through which the dispossessed musician reappropriates his work by signing it again, by *remarking* it. But the most striking phonogroove shown by the film is obviously the gramophonic engraving on the phantom's cheek, on his henceforth divided face: a kind of split-face (a scarred face or a "scarface" *avant la lettre*) that discloses the disfiguring violence inherent in all inscription, incision, indentation.[51]

The musician phantom crushed and branded by a vinyl press gives us an unusually powerful and horrifying image of the phonography or the indexation that extends and increases the possibilities of phonic marking by the manual clap.[52] This phonic scar that has been rendered visible constitutes the very condition of listening, which would not be able to come to life without the mortal mark of phonogrooving.

Death Records—this is the name of Swan's recording studio. The records of death. But we could also hear in this name the possibility that it is death who is recording, that it is death who is remembering: Death records. Similarly to what Echo did for Orpheus after his turnaround, it is with the perpetually repeated, lived, and relived experience of a loss that the ear opens itself up, perks up, hears, and listens. It is with the death of voices, phonogrooved in order to be buried or ventriloquized, that the ear lends itself, as we say, to what is to come. It is with the mute crypt of phonographic entombment that, like the investigating detective from Leroux's novel, the alert spy overhears the future.

Wozzeck at the Moment of his Death

Act 2, scene 4.

Like a mole or a sleuth, I discreetly enter the scene that unfolds right in front of me.

Wozzeck, in Alban Berg's opera, has just murdered Marie on the edge of the pond. After an incident at the tavern, he returns to the scene of his crime near the body. His knife is covered in blood. Wozzeck is himself covered in blood. He approaches the water. He wants to wash himself in the pond. He drowns.

We listen, but we hear less and less. He disappears, swallowed by the waves.

After so many different versions and adaptations, at the moment of his death Wozzeck appears to be merely a poor and weak reincarnation of Orpheus. A kind of exhausted and disenchanted transmigration or metempsychosis.

Wozzeck kills Marie, and Eurydice dies because of Orpheus. But whereas the latter kills the one he loves with his anxious love by not resisting the temptation to turn around to see her,

Wozzeck commits a heinous crime and becomes a murderer. He kills her with his own hands out of jealousy, whereas the other, the great singer, barely touches his lover from a distance with his magic voice. Finally, while Orpheus crosses the Styx without getting wet (carried by the power of this song that, before destroying Eurydice, liberated her by making her cross the watery frontier guarding the kingdom of the dead), Wozzeck drowns like a drunkard in his bathtub.

In truth, this Wozzeck makes for a pathetic Orpheus. Even if in death, like the other one who was dismembered and dispersed over the sky where the constellation of his lyre shines, he did have the right to another transformation (although certainly only a minor one) by which he is scattered little by little in the murky countryside that surrounds the pond. All that remains for Wozzeck from the orphic enchantment that could charm even the most savage animals is the ridiculous croaking of the toads who appear to observe his drowning indifferently.

But *when* does Wozzeck die? What is the exact *moment of his death*?[53]

Wozzeck drowns in the infinitely ascending movement of chromatic scales that are like musical waves that little by little die down on the surface of the pond that becomes immobile again. The Captain and the Doctor happen to pass by and listen. Wozzeck, however, does not appear to die at the precise moment when these two witnesses believe to hear a man dying. He could very well have died earlier. He could have been already dead.

Rather than the voices of these two witnesses then, it would be the croaking of the toads that bears witness to Wozzeck's moment of death.[54] And this croaking witnesses the death insofar as it *reappears*, such as it was announced at the very beginning of the scene. It would then be the *return* of the rumble of the amphibians, this strange device with a clock-like rhythm, that indicates the moment of Wozzeck's death.[55]

The croaking first appeared much earlier (m. 226) when Wozzeck was still alive, arousing in him the fear that "something is moving."[56] And, barely noticeably, the toads fall silent and withdraw from the sound stage: "Everything is calm and dead," (*alles still und tot*) Wozzeck notes more assuredly a few measures later.

But the croaking starts up again (m. 302). It returns after the long sound waves that represent the drowning, as if to mark its completion, as if to indicate that the water has once again closed up over the Wozzeck that it has swallowed. Here again, just like in *The Phantom of the Opera*, the return of the croaking punctuates, marks, and signals the death of the one who sings.

The mole, the sleuth, the listening guard that I am who over-hears this sordid scene, nevertheless does not yet see things clearly enough.

So what are we supposed to do with the clue provided by Berg himself, the orchestrator of the murderer's drowning? What are we supposed to make of these stage directions that, at the moment when Wozzeck utters the word "blood" over an excessively drawn-out interval, explicitly and laconically state: "He drowns" (*ertrinkt*)? Assuming that the moment of death can be determined and localized, shouldn't we pin-point it in this abyssal interval that makes Wozzeck's shrill voice lower into the inaudible range of his bass where it sinks straight to the bottom?

Indeed, the more I listen to this scene, the more the moment that I am tracking dilutes itself and dissolves in the flow of the music and the drama. In fact, itself drowned in the pool of blood that engulfs the whole scene, the moment loses its punctuality through a terrifying metonymic expansion that stretches from the moment when Wozzeck enters the water until the passing of the Captain and the Doctor.

Right before the stage directions that seem to indicate the moment of his death (*ertrinkt*), Wozzeck says: "I am bathing in blood—the water is blood." Through a metonymic contiguity, the water becomes blood according to the logic of a contamination that affects not only the fluids but also the solid objects, the countryside, in fact, little by little, the whole scenery. When a few measures earlier Wozzeck threw the knife into the pond, it was the moon that appeared "blood-red" through the clouds. As a result, this secret that Wozzeck wanted to hide at the bottom of the dark waters, this secret that threatened to betray his crime and that he has just washed, this secret is in the process of reinscribing itself everywhere. "So the whole world will blab my secret?"—he asks fearing that all the characters and props on stage, be they animate or inanimate, will begin to talk in the same collective voice like informers.

This generalized metonymy equally affects all the voices, which appear to be capable of replacing each other without any limitations, insofar as they are all touched by this contiguity just like fluids. Wozzeck himself begins by misrecognizing the echo of his own voice: "Ha! Who is calling? No—it was me." Later, during his chromatic drowning, when the Doctor and the Captain pass by, the former asks: "Can you hear?" And the latter responds: "It is the water in the pond. The water is calling." Even the water itself appears to have a voice that could be confused with the voice of the dying man. Finally, when the croaks return (m. 302), the Doctor, who is all ears, compares the collective voice of the toads to the sound of someone drowning: "That moan—like someone dying." Thus, we could conclude that at this moment Wozzeck was not yet dead. He was still moaning despite Berg's stage directions.

And it is here that, after having observed a short silence, the toads resume for a third time their chorus of croaks (m. 308–14). This time, however, reversing the order, it is now the Captain who asks: "Can you hear?—The croaking again." And the Doctor responds: "Fainter—now quite calm" (*Stiller, jetzt ganz still*).

We could then believe that it is at this moment, at this precise point that Wozzeck dies—really dies. But in passing, because of the play of contiguities and confusions, we have lost the *instant* of his death. Or, more precisely, his death has been extended, stretched out, distended in its punctuality in order to become a kind of span measured by the intermittent return of the toads. Postponed, Wozzeck's death appears to take place several times, like a dotted line.[57] Thanks to these metonymical substitutions that run through the whole scene, he dies three times rather than once: with the stage direction *ertrinkt*; with the return of the croaking; and with the Doctor's *jetzt ganz still*.

But what does Wozzeck exactly die of?

His drowning, marked by the toads, is something like a distant echo of Orpheus's descent into hell. While in the libretto it is of course water—the element of fusion—that swallows Wozzeck, in the score the saturation of the melodic space also appears to close up over him: He dies in the waves of the ascending chromatic scales that, by completely submerging all the musical interstices, by saturating them from bass to treble, drown out every possibility of singing. Thus, in these ascents that resemble groundswells sweeping away every note and every interval, it is not only Wozzeck who drowns in this inundation of all registers but also his voice and even melody in general. Wozzeck's drowning is also the stifling of singing itself, the slowing down and then the suffocation of all possible movement in the melodic dimension.

Wozzeck, therefore, dies of the submerging of singing. He dies in, of, and with the submersion of melodic space. Disenchanted Orpheus, his voice sinks into the Styx.

The return of the toads and their rhythmic croaking, rather than pinpointing the moment of his death (which remains forever drowned in the flux), punctuate this rise or flood that carries away and sinks singing, that swallows it up in what we could call a suicide of melody. The repetition of the croaking is actually the index of the closure of the melodic shut off in its own flood. So much so that in this scene of listening ("Can you hear?" the Captain asks), in this sequence where animal and human voices often appear to exchange themselves and substitute for each other (Wozzeck for the toads, the toads for Wozzeck), in this spectral scenery where all the different voices cross each other and every ear is wide open, in the end a kind of vast commutation is produced, an exchange of the two constitutive dimensions of music: melody and rhythm.[58]

After the submersion of singing, the return of the toads acts as the irruption of rhythm. An (almost) pure rhythm. It is an ostinato, a small horological device whose remarkable complexity brings into play the only temporal duration (the melodic movements are reduced to the minimum, as if compressed). First two, then three, finally four toads form as many voices in this chorus of varying periodicities.

This is how the music of the opera frames, isolates, encloses, or enfolds the space of singing in which Wozzeck dies. With the impassive, frozen, almost hieratic rhythm of the chorus of toads, the music delimits *as such* (by exhausting it and by enclosing it) the melodic field in and with which Wozzeck is drowned.[59]

How can we then hear Wozzeck's death? With what ears?

If it is in fact true that every act of listening worthy of the name is a punctuation of the flux or the flood that flows, then it is the toads that point out to me or indicate for me in advance the points of listening in this scene. The scene demands to be heard not with the eardrums of the frightened and confused passersby, the Doctor and the Captain; not with the submerged ears of the poor drowning man; but, if such a thing is possible, with the musical ears of the chorus of the toads who witness the drowning and thereby mark it as such. They punctuate it with their rhythmic croaking. We would have to listen to this death as it is listened to from the points of listening of a choir of toads who appear to have been always already there, waiting, in this scene where these men cross paths around the corpse of a woman—the murderer, the two witnesses, and myself, this listener that I am.

"The animal is there before me," Jacques Derrida wrote.[60] If the "bottomless gaze" of the animal that looks at me is "the point of view of the absolute other"; if it is, at the same time, "my primary mirror" in which I find myself reflected "deep within her eyes," then mutatis mutandis, Wozzeck's toads of death, these impassible and hieratic amphibians, are perhaps, in their rhythmic mechanical harmony, something like *the* alterity of the points of listening that watch out for me in advance so that I can reverberate or resound here in infinite echoes.[61]

The toads, in this fascinating sequence of scenes, would then be the *big ears of the other*: the ears, larger than me and always already preceding me, through which I listen; the ears, older than me and always already there, that listen to me as I listen.

Wozzeck, the Captain, the Doctor: They all whisper, and they all feel that they are being heard—and so do I, along with them—by this chorus of animals that wells up from the edges of the pond with its intermittent rhythms, its repeated points that punctuate, articulate, accentuate, mark, remark, and demarcate the death of singing, the suffocation or the deafening of musicality itself.

This croaking acts like the tracing of listening: It wells up, it emerges in advance from the musical stage like a dotted line made up of these mute points (*punctum surdum*) and, not unlike the blind spot of vision (*punctum caecum*), it is the very heart of listening. At the core of my listening to Wozzeck's death, there is this unheard-of and immemorial choir of punctuation. An archilistening, an overhearing that divides my listening from itself, that sweeps it up in an infinite reflection as it hurls it into an abyss.

A split-hearing, a dissonant listening, ruined or deconstructed in its own heart.

Adorno, the Informer

In this pursuit that has kept me on the trails of the metamorphoses of Orpheus and his mortal ear from the *Trackers* all the way to *Wozzeck*, in this following that seems to lead step by step toward a dissonant listening (a split-hearing), I knew very well that I would have to cross paths with another investigator who also appears to be following a trail: Adorno.

"The overwhelming impression which Wozzeck made on me that evening in Berlin revealed an inner involvement that I was hardly conscious of, even though it can be specified *down to the last detail*"—Benjamin wrote to Adorno on August 21, 1937, thanking the latter for sending him his monograph on Berg.[62] The two had attended a performance of *Wozzeck* together in Berlin on December 22, 1925. Their subsequent conversation appears to have left a deep impression on Benjamin, who still remembered it ten years later in a letter written on December 27, 1935, the day after Berg's death.[63]

Despite a few legible signs here and there, I will never know what they said to each other and whether they discussed the drowning, this scene of unheard-of listening. Yet I cannot help but think that not only did they discuss the work "down to the last detail," as Benjamin wrote, but that they also spoke about the detail as such, about its role, place, and function in music, in listening, and beyond. They were, after all, both great *detailers*.[64]

Incidentally, it was in reference to the subject of the detail that, on November 13, 1948, in an "open letter" published in the *Saturday Review of Literature*, Schoenberg gave voice to what resembles a legal complaint against Adorno:

> Sir,
>
> In his novel "Doctor Faustus" . . . Thomas Mann has taken advantage of my literary property. He has produced a fictitious composer [Adrian Leverkühn] as the hero of his book; and in order to lend him qualities a hero needs to arouse people's interests, he made him the creator of . . . my . . . "method of composing with twelve tones." . . . The informer was Mr. Wiesengrund-Adorno, a former pupil of my late friend Alban Berg. Mr. Adorno is very well acquainted with all the extrinsic details of this technique and thus was capable of giving Mr. Mann quite an accurate account of what a layman—the author—needs to tell another layman—the reader—to make him believe that he understands what it is about.[65]

What interests me here is not the accusation concerning artistic property (the confusion between fiction and reality that it bears witness to is quite naïve). Rather, beyond any concern with this charge, it is the status of the "informer" who was "acquainted with all the extrinsic details."

But what is a "musical detail"? And what does the spy do who, on request, provides such information, wholesale or retail, about the secrets of a musician's studio? In this affair, what is the role of this "detailer" whom we could call *listening philosopher* (*philosophe écoute*), referring to the old adjectival usage of the French word *écoute* (for example, in an expression like *sœur escoute*, which designates a "listening nun" charged with supervising a visiting room)?

As is well known, Adorno was asked by Thomas Mann to be a musical adviser for his novel. On December 30, 1945, Mann wrote the following:

> Dear Dr. Adorno
>   . . . I have brought the novel to the point where Leverkühn, at the age of thirty-five, in a first wave of euphoric inspiration, and in an incredibly short period of time, composes his principal work. . . . And my task now is to imagine and characterize the work in the most suggestive possible manner. . . . What I need are some significant *details* . . . which will create a plausible, indeed convincing, picture for the reader.[66]

Thus, what Mann expects from his "informer" (whom he called his "real secret councilor" in the dedication of the first edition of the novel) are *suggestive* details, information capable of producing an illusion.[67] As far as the use to which he wants to put this information is concerned, Mann speaks of the writing of the novel as if it involved a "montage technique" (*Montage-Technik*) to which he attributes a certain latent musicality: "Quotations of this kind have something musical about them, disregarding the innate mechanical quality."[68]

But to what extend would the *listening philosopher* subscribe to such an affirmation? Or rather: could the intelligence agent himself have been convinced of the intrinsically musical character of the details that he provided, that is to say, of the musicality that the details supposedly contained precisely *as details*?

When Adorno's thought takes musical listening for its object, it is itself caught up in an auditory dialectic of detail and totality. In this otodialectics of the musical ear that he deploys under the banner of "structural listening," meaning must emerge from the tension of the particular toward to the whole.

Speaking of an "education for an adequate listening," Adorno maintains that its goal is to guide the listener to "grasp the compositions in a structural manner," that is to say, to articulate their moments in such a way that "a contexture of meaning lights up" among them.[69] He then adds, as if he were giving a lesson in dialectics to Furtwängler over the phone: "The ideal . . . of structural listening is the necessary deployment of music from the detail [*Einzelne*] toward totality [*Ganze*], which in its turn determines the detail."

This is the premise from which Adorno will later develop his "instructions for listening to new music" as well as his reflections "on the musical employment of radio."[70] The call for an education of the ear that could teach it to "hear correctly" (which means "structurally") is the recurrent motif of this collection of essays edited in 1963 under the title "didactic writings on musical practice."[71] Adorno continuously returns to this topic, quite indefatigably. Discussing symphonies transmitted through the airwaves, he states: "We listen structurally . . . to the first measures of a movement of a classical symphony only at the moment when we listen to the final measure that redeems it [*einlöst*]."[72]

Likewise, in his recommendations for better listening to Schoenberg's music and the music of the second Viennese school that were broadcast over the radio, he told his listeners: "The listening that would be adequate . . . could be best described as structural. By recommending to listen . . . to what appears musically not only as the present but also—at the heart of the same composition—in its relation to the past and what is to come, we have already named an essential element of this ideal of listening."[73]

Two years later, in 1965, Adorno returned one more time, emphatically and insistently, to the necessity of structural listening. This time the occasion was a radio program called "Beautiful Passages" in which he intended to deliver to those listening a selection of his favorite moments taken from the works of composers ranging from Bach to Webern, by way of Mozart or Ravel.[74] Paradoxically, it is in the introduction of this autobiomusicographic anthology that we find the unquestionably most intransigent appeal for a sustained rather than a fragmented listening that goes beyond mere information gathering:

> The comprehension of music, of musical culture . . . amounts to the capacity to perceive the connections [*Zusammenhänge*] . . . like a meaningful whole [*sinnvolles Ganzes*]. This is what the concept of structural listening means, whose necessity announces itself today in an insistent and critical manner against the reign of the momentary, against this horrible naïveté. This pre-artistic atomized listening loses itself feebly and passively in the attraction of the instant, in the pleasant isolated sound, in the melody that one can take in at a glance and keep in memory.[75]

If these ears lost in the disintegration of the sonic flux are not or are no longer capable of grasping music by following it in its movement toward a meaningful whole (toward what Adorno also calls the "spiritual"), it is because, like the ears of a simple informer or a spy, they appear to be restricted to a mere gathering whose horizon and general plan escapes them. These are the ears that, like those of the one who would like to gather information everywhere, abandon their task of watchful surveillance at the threshold of a totality whose aim is not given to them, although it alone would be capable of transfiguring the collected details by retrospectively illuminating them with meaning.

In the same radio program, however, after this introduction that takes the form of a massive return to the order of structure, Adorno opens up a gap in his otherwise monolithic discourse on musical listening and the musical ear. In a dialectical reversal, his otology all of a sudden becomes quite welcoming toward the detail considered in itself and for itself. It goes as far as reading in it (not without some affinity with Thomas Mann's technique of citational montage) the promise of a musicality to come that can be anticipated only by an "exact imagination" (*exakte Phantasie*). The latter actually "discloses [*schliesst auf*] the richness of the detail that it dwells next to," and it confers on it "its own right." In the end, for Adorno, if the detail gathers in itself "so much substance," it is because "music itself, according to its idea, is more than culture, order, synthesis."

In his reflections "on the musical employment of radio," Adorno imagines in similar terms possible compositions to come that will be "truly adequate" to this medium.[76] In these works, he says, we should look everywhere for the contrast that "would extend the intensity of the singular moment and pierce . . . the cover of neutralization thrown over the music": "It would not be primarily the flux [*Verlauf*, literally the course of the music] that would found the meaning of a phenomenon, but its compositional emphasis granted to an acoustic sensorium just as rapid, versatile, and shrewd as the eyes of the regular viewer of detective films."[77]

By modeling itself on the eyes of the amateur viewer of crime and spy films (*Kriminalfilmen*), the ear of the radio listener seems capable of inventing a different relation between detail and structure. It is this *furtive* ear that we encounter again in the speech on "beautiful passages" where Adorno's otology takes an additional sigillographic turn: "Details [*Details*] of such dignity are like the seals guaranteeing the authenticity of a text. We could compare them to names. . . . The light of the beauty of details [*Einzelheiten*], once perceived, removes the brilliance with which culture has covered music."[78]

Under the seal of the detail that is hence more authentic than the whole, there is something like a hidden or sealed force. In opposition to the cultural usage that covers with its mantle the repertoire of works that have become classics, the hope of a musicality to come, beyond every possible synthesis, resides in this force. Being stamped by the details that it gathers, listening appears to lend an ear to the authenticity of what is unheard of.

It was still in the same program that Adorno evoked an idea from Alban Berg, who had been his composition teacher: The idea was to imagine a journal in which musical passages (that is to say, details) would be cited in the manner of Karl Kraus who, "as a punishment," cited excerpts from the idiotic nonsense of the press in his review *Die Fackel*.[79]

The practice of citation plays an equally important role in Adorno's contributions to *Doctor Faustus*, as we can see when we read the descriptions of the fictive compositions attributed to Leverkühn.[80] Being engaged in this information campaign through the history of music, Adorno the informer accepted that he was restricted to details without being able to master the whole of the novel and its form. The listening spy, a sonar working on behalf of the novelist, devoted himself and let himself be dedicated to details. To details irremediably detached from a whole that could subsume them. To details taken up and carried away in the discourse and the project of an other. Likewise, in his radio autobiography woven of beautiful passages, he countersigned in advance the texture that the other, the unknown listener, could weave with his favorite moments.

In short, the contexture of details, once again, will have been thought as a kind of weaving [*trame*] of the other's ear. And the outlines of another image of Adorno begin to emerge here: as a *listening philosopher*, that is to say, as a spy. It is another sketch of his ears, another oto-portrait in which, between the detail and the whole, his negative dialectics in its most Benjaminian accent crosses paths with the thought of deconstruction.[81]

Exit: J.D.'s Dream

Like so many others, the story of this spy could have started with a call, with a phone call. He would have heard the phone ring; he would have picked it up; and a voice at the end of the line would have revealed to him some information or entrusted him with a mysterious mission.

But this is not what happened. On the contrary, in Borges's short story "The Garden of Forking Paths," the story of the spy Yu Tsun opens in the aftermath of the interruption of the phone call [*dans l'après-coup de la coupure du coup de fil*]: ". . . and I hung up the receiver. Immediately afterwards, I recognized the voice that had answered in German. It was that of Captain Richard Madden."[1]

These are the first words, following a brief historical introduction, of the actual story, namely, of the "statement, dictated, reread and signed by Dr. Yu Tsun."[2] We do not know what happened before, immediately before, since the "first two pages of the document are missing." At the most, we can imagine Yu Tsun intensely listening to everything at the end of the line, careful *not to miss anything at all*, in short, *overhearing* every word, every noise, every moment of silence, even the smallest respiration that could provide him with a clue.

But it is after the suspension points, after the suspense of this overhearing striving for the totality of the whole that the moment of recognition occurs: ". . . and I hung up the receiver. *Immediately afterwards*, I recognized the voice."

This afterwardness [*après-coup*] is the time of the significant detail, of the clue that gives itself only in the echo of its return. The whole, its presence or its haunting, dissolves itself in order to give place in the delay of an echography to the detail that inscribes itself as it is enlarged.

In this phone call that he launches like a probe, like a reconnaissance or intelligence operation in an unknown land, the spy Yu Tsun resembles another who also listens to the voice at the other end of the line:

> And you, where do you "see" me when you speak to me, when you have me, as you say, on the telephone? . . . Me, I look out for the noises in the room around you, I try to surprise what you are looking at or looks at you, as if someone were hanging around, someone who might be me at times, there where you are, and often I stop paying attention to what you are saying so that the timbre alone resonates.[3]

Like Yu Tsun, the signatory of this postcard would like to *hear everything*. He ardently overhears. He looks out for the inaudible rumble of looks that escape him, before finishing by hanging up, as it were, even though he remains on the line: separating the voice from what it says, detaching it from itself by unhooking it from the meaning that it carries, he now listens only to the enlarged detail of the timbre. Hence it seems that the fragile voice becomes thicker, grows, inflates, insists, and consists: "The timbre alone resonates," and it has the tendency to become the whole by itself. It is in the process of becoming a part that is bigger than the whole.

It is at this point that, in the same postcard dated June 6, 1977, we see Orpheus enter the stage. A few lines later, I decipher a fragmented sentence, interspersed with blank spaces where the text is lost: After Eurydice's death, says the sender of these *Envois*, "Orpheus sings no more, he writes."[4]

No doubt, it is not an accident if the sender of this mail, right after having described himself as being in the very act of hanging up all the while remaining on the line, alludes to Orpheus's writing, to his phonography, that is, to the mark of his mortal ear simultaneously devoted to the loss of the whole and the echo of the detail.

Orpheus wanted to hear everything and see everything: He wanted to hear and see Eurydice as well as himself, the one who is following him as well as the one who is leading her. Until the moment when, thus overhearing, in a hyperbolic auditory doubt that touched even his own song, he let himself be caught by an offstage noise. He hung up in an excess of listening and, having lost the whole, he began to hear again in Echo's counterpoint the fragments and details that returned to him belatedly.

Escaping from this relentless overhearing, this panacoustic hypertension that does not want to lose anything at all from the whole, the detail, never immediately given, is in a certain sense infinitely finite in the echographies in which it is written and reinscribed. This is why all these different spies— Orpheus, Yu Tsun, and the others, including the signatory of *The Post Card*—pass it on and allow it to grow.

For them, after the fact, the part that expands in an abyssal manner grows until it becomes, after all, larger than the whole.

"One has to bring enormous attention to bear on each detail, enlarge it out of all proportion," Derrida wrote in *Right of Inspection*.[5] Enlargement, the blowup, hence becomes the watchword or the injunction formulated by one of the voices in this dialogue on photography considered as the art of the magnifier.[6]

As a result of this enlargement of details, of letting them grow, a certain implosion of the whole takes place.[7] It is this eruption of details in the aftermath of the after-all [*dans l'après-coup de l'après-tout*] that I in turn have tried to listen to by lending an ear to Orpheus and his avatars:[8] At the point where overhearing encounters its limit, where it ruins itself, it ends up announcing the deconstruction or the disenchantment of every "dream of a *general theory*," of a "complete inspection," of every panacoustic telelistening.[9] What remains, then, is this dissonant listening divided from itself that I have called "split-hearing"—which is not the listening to a dissonant interval or chord, but a listening that carries *in itself* its own dissonance, its unresolved duplicity, its fission that is not absorbed in a fusion.

Overhearing all the listening characters who accompanied me, spying on them as they listened to each other, I spied a certain diaphony at work, a hearing played out on several eardrums, among several voices in the hollow of the ear.

They listen to one another—ils s'écoutent: This is what I wanted to hear the whole time by following their traces and by overhearing them. *They look at one another—elles se regardent*: As Derrida repeated in *Right of Inspection*, with regard to two feminine characters who appeared in the photographs offered to his view:

> *They,* Claude and Camille, *look at one another* [*elles se regardent*]. Taken out of context such a sentence can mean three different things in French, it authorizes three senses:
>
> 1. *Elles se regardent*: One looks at the other, looking at the other who doesn't necessarily look back at the moment she is seen. . . .

2. *Elles se regardent*: Each one looks at *herself* in a mirror, without seeing the other. . . .

3. *Elles se regardent*: Both look at each other, their gazes intersecting, as one says, or being exchanged, each watching the other watch her, right in her eyes, with infinite speculation (I see the other seeing me see her, I look at you at the instant you watch me watching you).[10]

When they look at each other this way, reciprocally, under his scrutinizing gaze, there is no longer any photography properly speaking. The one who spies on them, external to the face-to-face of the two gazes, will never be able to see these eyes looking the other in the eyes: "But you will never see the look of the one looking—right in the eyes—at the look of the other, nor for that matter at your own."[11] For this violent staring of intersecting gazes, there are no proofs, or prints, or possible negatives for a third gaze.

But what can we say, after and following him, of these auricles that music or sound cinema represent for me? What can we say, for example, about Tamino and Pamina, Papageno and Papagena, who search for each other with their ears, who expect to hear each other, eardrum against eardrum. Would it be possible for me to listen to them listen to each other, to follow them as they prepare to hurl themselves into the abyss of each other's ears all the way to the phantasmatic enjoyment of perfect telelistening?

Of course, it does happen that I can, at the most, hear them listen, in the same way as he can see the heroines of his photonovel in the act of looking: Either I hear them lend an ear to the other, for example when Tamino or Papageno listen from a distance, or I hear one of them listen to himself, for example when Orpheus sings that he is singing or when his words are returned to him by Echo. But what I do not ever hear, of which there is no representation or possible experience for me, is the moment when their listenings meet and *hear one another* in telelistening. To put it differently, through these characters that music represents and in them represents me, I will never hear her, Music, as she listens to herself.

Like the spy Yu Tsun, the signatory of *The Post Card* himself also listened and overheard through the telephone. He extended his ears until they imploded, until he hung up the line, until there was nothing but this voice stripped bare of words, reduced to a part of itself, to its timbre that remains and nevertheless grows until it becomes the whole, all by itself the whole. He is now ready to drown, to dissolve, and to disappear in this detail enlarged beyond the whole: "I stop paying attention to what you are saying so that the timbre alone resonates . . . and then I am lying on my back, right on the ground as in the grand moments you remember, and I would accept death without a murmur."[12]

This telepheme that anticipates his death announces a hallucinatory scene that he would orchestrate later, in one of the rare pages that he dedicated to music. Otherwise, he said almost nothing about music, he who wrote so much about the ear, who would venture on so many paths, with his prudent risk-taking and his "dichemination" like no other.[13] I would like to lend an ear now to this unheard-of scene to hear one more time the doubling, the division, the split that divides overhearing at its most extreme point. So here is this scene, in the final cut that he gave to this musical dream of his survival or his salvation:

> the irresistible projection, the quasi-hallucination of a theatre, simultaneously visible and audible, of a plot in which the visible is carried away and transported by the time without time of music, and the scene . . . where I am—or where the I finds itself—dead but still there, and all those

(male and female) who are and will have been loved, all together, but everyone for himself or herself, as they listen together religiously to this music, which could be a song, but a song that is not dominated by an intelligible voice, a music whose author would not be the deceased (since he was already overcome and affected by it beforehand), but he would have elected it as if he had wanted to have had the genius to invent it, to compose it in order to offer it to them, so much so that in this speech ("here is the music, he said to himself, in which I would have liked to die, for which and with an eye to which in the end I would like to die"), the sadness of death or of the farewell would be then transformed from one moment to another into the overabundance of life. . . . The self dead yet raised by this music, by the unique coming of this music, here and now, in the same movement, the self dies by saying yes to death and as a result is resurrected, saying that I am reborn, but not without dying, I am reborn posthumously, the same ecstasy uniting in him death without return and resurrection, death and birth, the desperate greeting of an adieu without return and without salvation, without redemption but greeting the life of the other living in the secret sign and the exuberant silence of an overabundant life.[14]

In this probe sent in reconnaissance toward the future, toward death, everything happens as if the adjective *posthume* ("posthumous") became a verb conjugated in the first person in the present ("I posthume as I breathe," as he put it somewhere else).[15] There, on this stage, wherever it might be, he would have been in advance *safe, in music*.

But the anticipation in the dream appears to double itself by a contrary movement, what he called "the perversion of playback,"[16] since the soundtrack was chosen—"elected" as he puts it—to be replayed from over there, from this place without place where it posthumes [*ça posthume*], like a tele-phonogram returning from the future. In short, the flash-forward contains a kind of gramophony in advance inscribed in it that accompanies (permits or calls for the anticipation of) this *animation* of an "I" sent as a delegate to its own funeral.

He witnesses his own prerecorded death, and he spies on it.

"From wherever I am,"[17] he appears to be dreaming; "I" keep vigil and keep watch over his "here lies." Whereas his coffin is sealed in advance by a posthumous sigillography, his present listening is divided and double: It overhears, it traces, tracks, and marks in advance the unpredictable that is coming but in the form of a return or a reversion. It hurls itself straight ahead toward that from which it returns, moving backward or going the wrong way. Hence, the phonography of its ear, rushing toward "the imminence of the flash-back end," resembles this photographic compulsion that he described as being lodged in every living moment, inscribing there the haunting of a deadly accident: "a sort of compulsion to overtake each second, like one car overtaking another, doubling it rather, overprinting it with the negative of a photograph already taken with a 'delay' mechanism . . . terminable survival from which 'I see myself live' translates 'I see myself die.'"[18]

This would be the orphic bifurcation that would seal or sign the sigillary phonogram of his musical dream: Like the mortal ear of Orpheus, the dying ear that he calls would resemble a split screen, an eardrum in the shape of a split screen, the double tape of a diaphonic listening.

"This dream that I dream," he said himself, "would not be either from Apollo or from Dionysus." It would not be either the dream of form or of structure, either of trance or the pure enjoyment of the passing moment. This dream, he wrote citing Nietzsche, was about being "in a drunken state and at the same time being posted behind myself like a lookout."[19]

We are dealing here with an eardrum irremediably divided or split between two paths that bifurcate yet follow each other like shadows. In short, this dissonant or "dicheminated" split-hearing toward which Orpheus's path leads, as J.D. has foreseen in a dream, belongs to an ear overtaking and doubling the other at every moment. It is as if an interminable secret conversation between two voices infinitely split every nevertheless finite second of listening.[20]

This is how I in fact listen to them as they listen, listen to each other, and listen to themselves in order to survey or hear each other or themselves: Figaro and Susanna, the Count and the Countess, Orpheus and Eurydice, Tamino and Pamina, Papageno and Papagena, or even Harry, Winslow, Wozzeck, Professor Armstrong, and Yu Tsun, as well as all the other moles who, ever since the biblical Jericho, occupy the places of an immemorial *topmology* of listening.[21]

And even when they all disappear, when their phantoms dissipate, there remain, in their places, their places themselves. Between these, overhearing infinitely divides listening by carving in it the otographic groove of the ear of the other.

His ear in the hollow of my ear.

NOTES

(No) More Ears: A Preface to the English-Language Edition

1. *All Ears: The Aesthetics of Espionage* was first published in French as *Sur Écoute: Esthétique de l'espionage* in 2007 by Éditions de Minuit.

2. The first was *Listen: A History of Our Ears*, which was published in French as *Écoute: Une histoire de nos oreilles* in 2001 by Éditions de Minuit. Charlotte Mandell's English translation was published in 2008 by Fordham University Press.

3. Among other places, Derrida discusses the quasi transcendental in the following passage from *Resistances of Psychoanalysis*: "A quasi-transcendental law of seriality that could be illustrated . . . each time, in fact, that the transcendental condition of a series is, paradoxically, a part of that series" (Jacques Derrida, *Resistances of Psychoanalysis*, trans. Peggy Kamuf, Pascale-Anne Brault, and Michael Naas [Stanford: Stanford University Press, 1998], 79).

4. In *Memoirs of the Blind*, Derrida himself spoke of a "powerlessness" of the eye that "gives to the experience of drawing its *quasi-transcendental* resource" (Jacques Derrida, *Memoirs of the Blind: The Self-Portrait and Other Ruins*, trans. Pascale-Anne Brault and Michael Naas [Chicago: University of Chicago Press, 1993], 44).

1. See "Les grandes oreilles de Tony Blair: La polémique sur les écoutes visant Kofi Annan," *Libération*, February 28–29, 2004.
2. Duncan Campbell, *Surveillance électronique planétaire* (Paris: Allia, 2001).
3. H. Keith Melton, *The Ultimate Spy Book* (New York: Dorling Kindersley, 1996).
4. Ibid., no page number.
5. Ibid.
6. Ibid.
7. Ibid., 18.
8. Sun Tzu, *The Art of War*, trans. Samuel B. Griffith (New York: Oxford University Press, 1971), 145–46.
9. *The Holy Bible: New Revised Standard Version with Apocrypha* (New York: Oxford University Press, 1989).
10. [Translator's note: The semantic ambiguity of the French expression *s'écouter* will be very important for Szendy's argument. The most common usage refers to the way something should be listened to. But the reflexive pronoun opens up other possibilities as well: On the one hand, in a particular context it could mean that several people *listen to each other*; on the other hand, it can also mean that someone is *listening to himself or herself*.]
11. In this sense, the *double agent* would be a figure of what Jacques Derrida calls *autoimmunity* (in "Faith and Knowledge" as well as in *Rogues: Two Essays on Reason*). In a different context and in different terms, the saxophonist Wayne Shorter seems to be speaking of the same self-protection against the force of sound, inasmuch as it is in advance listened to and anticipated in improvisation, when he declares: "sound is something that you have to fight against. It is *your own enemy*." See François-René Simon, "Le Monde selon Wayne," *Jazz Magazine* 544 (January 2004), emphasis added. See Jacques Derrida, "Faith and Knowledge: The Two Sources of 'Religion' at the Limits of Reason," in *Acts of Religion*, ed. Gil Anidjar (New York: Routledge, 2002), 42–101; and Jacques Derrida, *Rogues: Two Essays on Reason*, trans. Pascale-Anne Brault and Michael Naas (Stanford: Stanford University Press, 2005).

12. Quoted by Jean Lévi in his commentary on *The Art of War*. See Sun Tzu, *L'Art de la guerre*, trans. Jean Lévi (Paris: Hachette Littératures, 2000), 295, emphasis added.

Discipline and Listen

1. Sun Tzu, *The Art of War*, trans. Samuel B. Griffith (New York: Oxford University Press, 1971), 149.
2. This is what my friend Gil Anidjar (who by the way devoted a few beautiful pages to listening to spectral voices in Jewish mysticism) whispered to me one day, not without some malice. See Gil Anidjar, *"Our Place in al-Andalus": Kabbalah, Philosophy, Literature in Arab Jewish Letters* (Stanford: Stanford University Press, 2002).
3. Roland Barthes, "Listening," in *The Responsibility of Forms: Critical Essays on Music, Art, and Representation*, trans. Richard Howard (Berkeley: University of California Press, 1991), 245.
4. For these etymologies of the French word *écoute*, I will also refer to Jean Lauxerois's article "'À bon entendeur': Petite note sur l'écoute structurelle," *Circuit* 14, no. 1 (2003): 87–102.
5. Freud defines this auditory hyperesthesia as "an oversensitiveness to noise—a symptom which is undoubtedly to be explained by the innate intimate relationship between auditory impressions and fright." Sigmund Freud, "On the Grounds for Detaching a Particular Syndrome from Neurasthenia under the Description 'Anxiety Neurosis,'" in *The Standard Edition of the Complete Psychological Works of Sigmund Freud*, trans. James Strachey et al. (London: Hogarth Press, 1962), 3:92.
6. [Translator's note: In the rest of the text, the expression *surécoute* (in all its forms) will be consistently translated as "overhearing." Since in the rest of the book the English term "overhearing" will appear only when it is a translation of *surécoute*, the reader will always be able to hear in the background the counterpoint of Szendy's neologism.]
7. *The Concise Oxford Dictionary of Current English* defines "overhear" as "hear as eavesdropper or as unperceived or unintentional listener."
8. James Joyce, *Finnegans Wake* (New York: Penguin, 1976), 70.
9. Ibid., 71.

10. *L'orecchio di Dionigi*, as it is called in Italian, is a sort of cave (an old quarry located in the *Parco Archeologico* of Syracuse) whose popular name appears to have come from Caravaggio who, when he visited it in 1586, compared its entrance to a human ear. See Dörte Zbikowski, "The Listening Ear: Phenomena of Acoustic Surveillance," in *CTRL [Space]: Rhetorics of Surveillance from Bentham to Big Brother*, ed. Thomas Levin (Cambridge: MIT Press, 2002), 37.

11. Henry Swinburne, *Travels in the Two Sicilies, in the Years 1777, 1778, 1779, and 1780* (London: T. Cadell & P. Elmsky, 1790), 105.

12. Ibid.

13. Athanasius Kircher, *Musurgia universalis* (Rome, 1650), 2:291.

14. Dörte Zbikowski mentions other examples of what she calls "whispering galleries": St. Paul's Cathedral in London; the old Hall of Representatives of the Capitol building in Washington, D.C.; and the Agrigento Cathedral in Sicily. Deploring the lack of reliable sources on this subject, she also cites a source according to which Catherine de' Medici supposedly had installed a similar listening device in the walls of the Louvre at the time of the St. Bartholomew's Day massacre. She suggests that the expression "the walls have ears" might have had its origins here. See Zbikowski, "Listening Ear," 38, 41.

15. Italo Calvino, *Under the Jaguar Sun*, trans. William Weaver (New York: Harcourt Brace, 1990), 38.

16. See Michel Foucault, *Discipline and Punish: The Birth of the Prison*, trans. Alan Sheridan (New York: Vintage, 1995). The full title of Bentham's plans, published in the form of letters, is the following: *Panopticon; or, The inspection-house: containing the idea of a new principle of construction applicable to any sort of establishment, in which persons of any description are to be kept under inspection.*

17. Jeremy Bentham, *The Panopticon Writings* (New York: Verso, 2011), 34.

18. Foucault, *Discipline and Punish*, 201–2. See also the French version of Bentham's work translated by Étienne Dumont under the title *Mémoire sur un nouveau principe pour construire des maisons d'inspection, et nommément des maisons de force* (Paris: Mille et une nuits, 2002), 12–13. The original version was read to the National Assembly and was published with an introductory letter by the author in 1791.

19. Bentham, *Panopticon Writings*, 36–37.

20. Ibid., 94.

21. Foucault, *Discipline and Punish*, 317.

22. See Bentham's sixth letter as well as Dumont's French version: "One of the great collateral advantages of this plan is that it places the deputy inspectors, the subalterns of all kinds, under the same inspection as the prisoners: nothing can pass among them that is not seen by the chief inspector. In ordinary prisons, a prisoner hurt by his guards has no means to appeal to the humanity of his superiors. If he is ignored or oppressed, he must suffer. But in the Panopticon, the eye of the master is everywhere. There is no subaltern tyranny possible here, no secret humiliations. . . . Furthermore, the curious public, travellers, the friends and parents of the prisoners, the acquaintances of the inspector and other prison officers who, all motivated by different reasons, will come to increase the force of the salutary principle of surveillance and will inspect the chiefs like the chiefs inspect all their subordinates. This grand committee of the public will perfect all the establishments that will be submitted to its vigilance and penetrating inspection." Dumont, *Mémoire sur un nouveau principe*, 14–16.

23. Sigmund Freud, "A Case of Paranoia Running Counter to the Psycho-Analytic Theory of the Disease," in *The Standard Edition of the Complete Psychological Works of Sigmund Freud,* trans. and ed. James Strachey (London: Hogarth, 1961), 14:269.

24. Ibid., emphasis added.

25. Peter Szendy, *Listen: A History of Our Ears*, trans. Charlotte Mandell (New York: Fordham University Press, 2008).

26. Lorenzo Da Ponte, *Memoirs*, trans. Elisabeth Abbott (New York: New York Review of Books, 2000), 129–30.

27. Pierre-Augustin Caron de Beaumarchais, *The Figaro Trilogy: The Barber of Seville, The Marriage of Figaro, The Guilty Mother*, trans. David Coward (Oxford: Oxford University Press, 2008), 192.

28. Quoted by Wye Jamison Allanbrook in his remarkable study *Rhythmic Gesture in Mozart*, on which I rely heavily here. See Allanbrook, *Rhythmic Gesture in Mozart: Le Nozze di Figaro and Don Giovanni* (Chicago: University of Chicago Press, 1983), 33.

29. Allanbrook speaks of a "revolution of the danceless dance" underlining that "the middle class as we think of it today, the bourgeoisie, does not have its own [choreographic] expression until the advent of the contredanse." Ibid., 60, 69.

30. "The audience in the court of Louis XIV watched individual performances, each straining to the utmost to perform the correct expressive gestures of their dance. The audience in a dance hall (most not in actuality spectators, but participants restively waiting their turn) witnessed a mass of gay but obedient dancers following the leader about the room, points in an abstract human geometry." Ibid., 62.

31. In certain passages, the overhearing of one character by others is also inscribed in the rhythmical structures of the work. Thus, during the second duettino, when Figaro evokes the proximity of the masters ("in two steps," "in three bounds"), his song adopts the light cadence of a contredanse. But his imitation of the bells interrupts and turns this contredanse into a march, more threatening due to its clearly marked steps. Moreover, the beat of this march is *contracted* into three measures (instead of the usually expected four) according to a constriction that literally gives us to hear the proximity evoked by the words of the song (*due passi, tre salti*).

32. "The ear, the organ of fear, could have evolved as greatly as it has only in the night and twilight of obscure caves and woods, in accordance with the mode of life of the age of fear" (Friedrich Nietzsche, *Daybreak: Thoughts on the Prejudices of Morality*, ed. Maudemarie Clarke and Brian Leiter [Cambridge: Cambridge University Press, 1997], 253, translation modified).

33. Ibid.

34. See, in particular, the following passage in *Introduction to the Sociology of Music* devoted to the "anthropological difference between ear and eye," where Adorno seems to fix vision and hearing in an opposition that is physiological in nature: "The ear is passive. The eye is covered by a lid and must be opened; the ear is open and must not so much turn its attention toward stimuli as seek protection from them." Theodor W. Adorno, *Introduction to the Sociology of Music*, trans. E. B. Ashton (New York: Seabury Press, 1976), 51.

35. Roland Barthes, *The Responsibility of Forms: Critical Essays on Music, Art, and Representation*, trans. Richard Howard (Berkeley: California University Press, 1991), 245.

36. Ibid.

37. Ibid., 258.

38. Ibid., 247.

39. Ibid., 247, 248.

40. Ibid., 248, 249. "The best legend which accounts for the birth of language is the Freudian story of the child who mimes his mother's absence and presence as a game during which he throws away and pulls back a spool attached to a thread: he thereby creates the first symbolic game, but he also creates rhythm. Let us imagine this child listening for noises which can tell him of the mother's desired return: he is in the first stage of listening, that of indices; but when he stops directly supervising the appearance of the index and begins miming its regular return himself, he is making the awaited index into a sign: he shifts to the second stage of listening, which is that of meaning: what is listened for is no longer the *possible* (the prey, the threat, the object of desire which occurs without warning), it is the *secret*: that which, concealed in reality, can reach human consciousness only through a code, which serves simultaneously to encipher and to decipher that reality." Ibid., 249.

41. Ibid., 258.

42. Ibid.

43. Ibid., 259.

44. According to Barthes, the third listening is "supposed to develop in an inter-subjective space where 'I am listening' also means 'listen to me.'" Ibid., 246.

45. We should try to understand the significance of Barthes's expression "by deconstructing itself, listening is externalized" beyond what the final lines of the essay propose in terms of a decidedly binary logic of liberation: "Freedom of listening is as necessary as freedom of speech. . . . [Listening] is finally like a little theater on whose stage those two modern deities, one bad and one good, confront each other: power and desire." Ibid., 259–60.

46. Gilles Deleuze, "Postscript on Societies of Control," in *Negotiations*, trans. Martin Joughin (New York: Columbia University Press, 1997), 177–82.

47. Barthes, *Responsibility of Forms*, 259.

48. Deleuze, "Postscript on Societies of Control," 177–78.

49. Ibid., 178–179.

50. Borrowing Gilbert Simondon's vocabulary, Deleuze calls these relations "metastable." According to Deleuze, in disciplinary societies "power both amasses and individuates, that is, it fashions those over whom it's exerted into a body of people and molds the individuality

of each member of that body." In societies of control, in contrast, "Individuals become '*dividuals*,' and masses become samples, data": What tends to replace "individual or numbered bodies" is "'dividual' matter to be controlled." Ibid., 179–80, 182.

51. [Translator's note: The French expression *point d'écoute* is sometimes translated into English as "point of audition." At least this is the common translation of Michel Chion's definition of the term. In order to distinguish Szendy's understanding of the term from Chion's, I consistently translate it as "point of listening." See Michel Chion, *Film, a Sound Art*, trans. Claudia Gorbman (New York: Columbia University Press, 2009), 485–86.]

52. In the Anglo-Saxon vocabulary of film and video, the verb *to pan* (an abbreviation of "panorama") designates a horizontal movement of the camera, that is to say, of the point of view. We must also note here that Bentham's panoptic plan and the invention of Panorama (by the English Robert Barker) are contemporary events that both occurred in 1787. The acoustic equivalent in the techniques of stereo- or quadriphonic spatialization of a recording is obtained through an apparatus called the *panpot* (an abbreviation of "panoramic potentiometer") that allows the creation of the illusion that the source of the sound moves in a circle within the auditory field.

53. See Adorno's *Introduction to the Sociology of Music* as well as my critical reading of it in *Listen: A History of Our Ears*.

54. Wilhelm Furtwängler, "Bach," in *Furtwängler on Music*, trans. Ronald Taylor (Hants: Scolar Press, 1991), 27–28, translation modified. [Translator's note: The available English translation distorts the original to a degree that renders it all but useless in the present context. See also "Bach," in Wilhelm Furtwängler, *Ton und Wort: Aufsätze und Vorträge, 1918 bis 1954* (Wiesbaden: F. A. Brockhaus, 1958), 215.]

55. [Translator's note: The French expression *la musique (s')écoute elle-même* is rich with ambiguity. First, it implies that "music itself listens" (*la musique écoute*). At the same time, it also implies that this primary listening of music (which is a listening carried out by music) is nevertheless still a listening to music: "Music is listened to" (*la musique s'écoute*). Finally, as a third step, we have to introduce the self-reflexive dimension: This music that simultaneously listens and is listened to actually listens to itself (*la musique (s')écoute elle-même*).]

56. Wilhelm Furtwängler, "Heinrich Schenker: A Contemporary Problem," *Sonus* 6, no. 1 (1985): 4–5.

57. The exhibition Entartete Musik ("Degenerate Music")—organized by Hans Severus Ziegler, the director of the Weimar National Theater—took place in Düsseldorf in 1938 to celebrate the first "musical festival of the Reich." See Albrecht Dümling and Peter Girth, *Entartete Musik: Eine kommentierte Rekonstruktion* (Düsseldorf: Der Kleine Verlag, 1988). I will not go into the question of Furtwängler's position during the Second World War: He has been sufficiently criticized for having stayed in Germany. In fact, he himself tried to explain this by claiming that, every time he had the chance, he tried to defend Jewish musicians, and this way, he attempted to embody what he considered to be the most courageous form of resistance, an internal resistance.

58. Wilhelm Furtwängler, *Notebooks, 1924–1954*, trans. Shaun Whiteside (New York: Quartet Books, 1989), 139, first emphasis in original, second emphasis added.

59. Luca Cerchiari, *Jazz e fascismo* (Palermo: L'Epos, 2003).

60. Julio Cortázar, "Pursuer," in *Blow-Up and Other Stories*, trans. Paul Blackburn (New York: Collier, 1963), 196.

61. Since the era of bebop, quite a number of jazz compositions (that are not standards borrowed from Broadway or love songs) have evoked the chase: "Chasing the Train," by John Coltrane; "Chasing the Bird," by Charlie Parker; James Carter's album titled *Chasing the Gipsy*, which is an homage to Django Reinhardt, who himself often played the song "Chasing Shadows" under the French title "Mirages."

62. Robin Rimbaud, "Scanner: Cartographier les villes," in *Sonic Process: Une nouvelle géographie des sons*, ed. Christophe Kihm (Paris: Centre Pompidou, 2002), 240–45. This secret enjoyment inevitably evokes in me a childhood game that repeats something from Freud's primal scene of the fantasy of listening: I specifically recall the pleasure that I took in recording with a small tape recorder family conversations and disputes in Budapest, as well as the bouts of laughter when I insatiably replayed the tape.

63. Chion, *Film, a Sound Art*, 291.

64. Ibid., 293–94.

65. Thomas Levin, "Rhetoric of the Temporal Index: Surveillant Narration and the Cinema of 'Real Time,'" in *CTRL [Space]: Rhetorics of*

Surveillance from Bentham to Big Brother, ed. Thomas Levin, Ursula Frohne, and Peter Weibel (Cambridge: MIT Press, 2002), 582.

66. Ibid., 583.

67. Embedded listening "refers to those situations where a character in a film listens . . . , thus foregrounding the spectator's own experience in the movie theater." Chion, *Film, a Sound Art*, 476. As for me, in *Listen: A History of Our Ears*, I spoke of "listening to listening" (99–128).

68. Michel Foucault described with these words ("the place of the king") the structure of the perspective in his analysis of Velasquez's *Meninas*: "The occupier of that ambiguous place in which the painter and the sovereign alternate, in a never-ending flicker, as it were, is the spectator." Michel Foucault, *The Order of Things: An Archaeology of the Human Sciences* (New York: Routledge, 2005), 335–36.

69. This is the reason why he is simultaneously listening and listened to, an ambiguity that evokes the fantasy of Freudian listening.

Underground Passage: The Mole in Its Burrow

1. [Translator's note: Szendy is playing here on the semantic ambiguity of the word *écoute*. He is trying to put to use several meanings of the term based on his earlier etymological inquiries: (1) the archaic meaning of *une écoute* is something like a "listening guard"; (2) at the same time, however, *l'écoute* designates listening itself (and in the case of *une écoute*, a specific form of listening); (3) finally, it is also used to designate auditory surveillance. In the rest of the chapter, these three meanings (listener/listening/surveillance) will be preserved by translating the term as "listening," "listener," "listening guard," or "auditory surveillance" depending on the context.]

2. Franz Kafka, "The Burrow," in *The Complete Stories*, ed. Nahum N. Glatzer (New York: Schocken, 1972), 325–59.

3. As a synonym of *Bau*, the word *Werk* appears in the text: for example, when the narrator discusses this "complete work of small zigzags" [*ein volles kleines Zickzackwerk*] that was the first part of the construction, the "debut work" [*Erstlingswerk*] of its architect or animal author. See ibid., 331, 332. Translations modified.

4. Ibid., 326.

5. [Translator's note: Szendy's neologism *taupologie* is a pun that combines "topology" with the French word for "mole" (*une taupe*). Hence the translation, *topmology*, or "top-mole-ogy."]
6. Kafka, "Burrow," 333–34.
7. Ibid., 326.
8. Umberto Eco, "L'Anopticon," in *Il secondo diario minimo* (Milan: Bompiani, 1992), 176.
9. Kafka, "Burrow," 327.
10. Ibid.
11. Ibid., 343.
12. Ibid.
13. Ibid., 343–44.
14. "I merely disfigure the walls of my burrow, scratching hastily here and there without taking time to fill up the holes again." Ibid., 348.
15. [Translator's note: The French saying "L'imagination est la folle du logis" literally means that the imagination is the madwoman of the house. In a more general sense, it denotes the inferiority of the imagination in relation to other faculties of the mind. In this context, however, *logis* also works as a translation of the German *Bau*.]
16. "I intend now to alter my methods. I shall dig a wide and carefully constructed trench in the direction of the noise and not cease from digging until, independent of all theories, I find the real cause of the noise. Then I shall eradicate it, if that is within my power, and if it is not, at least I shall know the truth. That truth will bring me either peace or despair, but whether the one or the other, it will be beyond doubt or question." Kafka, "Burrow," 348.
17. Ibid., 345.

In the Footsteps of Orpheus

1. [Translator's note: the French word *limier,* just like the English "sleuth," designates both a detective and a bloodhound.]
2. Sophocles, *Les Limiers*, ed. and trans. Paul Masqueray (Paris: Les Belles Lettres, 1934). The Greek title *Ichneutae* designates "humans or animals who follow the path of a trace" or, according to another translation proposed by Reinach, "trackers." [Translator's note: For a recent English translation, see *Sophocles II: Ajax, The Women of*

Trachis, Electra, Philoctetes, The Trackers, ed. and trans. Mark Griffith, Glenn W. Most, David Grene, Richmond Lattimore (Chicago:
University of Chicago Press, 2013). In what follows, I provide cita-
tions to this English translation, but I will modify them to closely
follow the French translation that Szendy provides, since the argument often specifically depends on these translations.]

3. *Sophocles II*, 289. Translation modified.

4. Paul Masqueray comments: "In this verse, . . . for the first twelve
lines only the first syllables survive. We believe that the Satyrs are
trying to convince each other to follow the thief of Apollo's cattle.
They want to earn the double reward that the god promised them."
Les Limiers, 236. My translation.

5. *Sophocles II*, 289. Translation modified.

6. Anne Mahoney's translation based on the text edited by Arthur S.
Hunt, available at www.perseus.tufts.edu.

7. *Les Limiers*, 237; *Sophocles II*, 290–91.

8. "*Chorus Leader*: Queen of this domain, powerful Cyllene . . . tell us,
what is this noise that speaks to us, and who among the mortals can
express himself this way? *Cyllene:* . . . the child who dwells in this
underground cave . . . As for the trembling voice coming from the
invisible instrument that so astounded you and whose origins you
ask me about: he had the idea all alone to make it, in one day, from
an overturned carcass . . . of a dead animal . . . he is making it
resound down underground . . . *Chorus Leader*: How could I believe
that from a dead animal such a voice might ring forth? *Cyllene*:
Believe me; when it was dead, the animal had a voice; when it was
alive, it was mute. . . . *Chorus Leader*: But what part of its body
speaks: the inside or the outside? . . . What do you call it? *Cyllene*:
The child calls this animal turtle; and the part of its body that speaks,
he calls lyre. [*Nine mutilated verses follow here.*] This is how the child
found the means to give voice to a dead animal." *Les Limiers*, 242–48;
Sophocles II, 296–97.

9. Arturo Schwartz, *The Complete Works of Marcel Duchamp* (New
York: Thames and Hudson, 1969), 462.

10. As Jean-Luc Nancy put it recently in *Listening*: "Sound has no hidden
face; it is all in front, in back, and outside inside, *inside-out* in relation to the most general logic of presence as appearing, as phenom-
enality or as manifestation, and thus as the visible face of a presence

subsisting in self. Something of the theoretical and intentional scheme tuned to optics vacillates around it." Jean-Luc Nancy, *Listening*, trans. Charlotte Mandell (New York: Fordham University Press, 2007), 13–14.

11. Giambattista della Porta, in his *Magiae naturalis* published in Naples in 1589, imagined the following experiment (which is not unlike the "echotectonic" apparatus described by Athanasius Kircher a century later in his *Musurgia universalis*): "If any man shall make leaden pipes exceeding long, two or three hundred paces long (as I have tried) and shall speak in them some or many words, they will be carried true through those pipes and be heard at the other end, as they came from the speaker's mouth. Wherefore if that voice goes with time, and hold entire, if an man as the words are spoken shall stop the end of the pipe, and that is at the other end shall do the like, the voice may be intercepted in the middle, and be shut up as in a prison. And when the mouth is opened, the voice will come forth, as out of his mouth that spoke it." John Baptista Porta, *Natural Magick* (London: Thomas Young and Samuel Speed, 1658), 385–86.

12. In 1988, Christian Marclay created an object titled *Secret*: It is a metal master disk on which, as he put it, "something is recorded," but a padlock surrounding the grooves and passing through the central hole prevents us from ever hearing it. (For the connections between Duchamp's *With Secret Noise* and Marclay's *Secret*, see Russell Ferguson, "The Variety of Din," in *Christian Marclay* [Los Angeles: UCLA Hammer Museum, 2003], 32–33.)

13. Cited in *Écouter par les yeux: Objets et environnements sonores* (Paris: Musée d'Art Moderne, 1980), 106.

14. Beyond the deep bass of the editor(s) of the book of Joshua, we can also hear the voice of Kant's baritone: "[Music] extends its influence further (into the neighborhood) than is required" (Immanuel Kant, *Critique of the Power of Judgment*, trans. Paul Guyer [Cambridge: Cambridge University Press, 2001], 207); as well as Hegel's tenor: "The ear, on the contrary . . . listens to the result of the inner vibration of the body through which what comes before us is . . . the first and more ideal breath of the soul" (*Aesthetics: Lectures on Fine Art*, trans. T. M. Knox [Oxford: Oxford University Press, 1998], 2:890).

15. In response to François Truffaut's question "Had you seen *M*?," Hitchcock responds with the light suspicion of feigned ignorance:

"Yes. I don't remember it too well. Wasn't there a whistling man in it?" Truffaut interjects: "Yes, that was Peter Lorre!" See François Truffaut, *Hitchcock* (New York: Simon and Schuster, 1967), 61.

16. Bernard Herrmann, who wrote several pieces of music for Hitchcock, reorchestrated for the 1956 remake the cantata *The Storm Cloud* that Arthur Benjamin composed for the first version of the film in 1934. We can also see, right before this scene, Herrmann's name ("Bernard Herrmann conducts") on a poster by the entrance of Albert Hall. See Jean-Pierre Eugène, *La Musique dans les films d'Alfred Hitchcock* (Paris: Dreamland, 2000), 80.

17. In his conversations with Truffaut, Hitchcock recounts: "The idea for the cymbals was inspired by a cartoon, or rather by a comic strip that appeared in a satirical magazine like *Punch*. . . . They called him "The One Note Man," and the story of that little fellow, waiting to play his one note, gave me the idea of getting a suspense effect from the cymbals." Truffaut, *Hitchcock*, 62–63.

18. Michel Chion, in his *Film, a Sound Art* (New York: Columbia University Press, 2009), speaks about these phantom or negative sounds "that the image suggests but we don't hear" due to a "masking effect" (483, 480).

19. The semantic oscillation of the French verb *dépister* fascinates me: It primarily means to hunt for game by following its trail ("dépister un sanglier," for example, is to hunt for boar) and, by analogy, to find someone by following his or her traces ("dépister un criminel" is to hunt down a criminal). But in another sense, it also means to throw off the track, to foil, to set someone on a false trail ("dépister la police" means to mislead police, while "dépister les soupçons" is to divert suspicions).

20. I follow Denis Stevens's edition: *L'Orfeo, favola in musica da Claudio Monteverde . . .* (London: Novello, 1968). As far as Striggio's libretto is concerned, I cite it as it appears in *Libretti d'opera italiani, dal Seicento al Novecento*, ed. Giovanna Gronda and Paolo Fabbri (Milan: Monadori, 1997).

21. That is to say, outside the space of musical representation properly speaking: *Qui si fa strepito dietro alla scena*, as the stage directions of the libretto instruct us: "There is a noise behind the set." Gronda and Fabbri, *Libretti d'opera italiani*, 42.

22. In the famous aria of the third act, *Possente spirto*, the supplication that Orpheus addresses to Charon is first accompanied by two violins, then by two *cornetti*, and finally by a harp (*arpa doppia*, bars 193 ff., and bars 271 ff.). While the violins and the *cornetti* respond to Orpheus's song by echoing each other (by imitating each other), the harp engages in a play of melodic inversions: Its ascending motifs *turn into* descending figures and vice versa. Furthermore, these reversals happen immediately (one measure) after the occurrence of the verb *voltare* in the libretto: *A lei volt'ho 'l cammin*, Orpheus sings: "It is toward her [toward Eurydice] that I *turned* my steps [literally: my path]."

23. Through Echo's voice *Ahi pianto* ("Oh! Weep") becomes *hai pianto* ("you have wept"): I analyzed these anagrammatic puns (that are not always respected by the various editions and translations of the libretto) in "Sous reserve: De la rature chez Monteverdi, Vinteuil et quelques autres," in *Musica practica: Arrangements et phonographies de Monteverdi à James Brown* (Paris: Harmattan, 1997), 37.

24. See Barry Gifford's foreword in *The Complete Lynch*, ed. David Hughes (London: Virgin Books, 2001), 6: "*Lost Highway* which I would like to call *Orpheus and Eurydice Meet Double Indemnity*."

25. I borrow the word "telepheme" from Michel Chion, who uses it to designate a "scene of a telephone conversation in a film." He also classifies it into several types like the split screen ("allowing us to see and hear both speakers") as well other cases "that are deliberately aberrant or paradoxical." Chion, *Film, a Sound Art*, 494.

26. Walter Benjamin, "(Tele)Pathie," in *Gesammelte Schriften*,,ed. Rolf Tiedemann and Hermann Schweppenhauser (Frankfurt: Suhrkamp, 1991), 6:187–88.

27. In "Dreams and Occultism," Freud illustrates telepathy with the following example: "Person A may be the victim of an accident or may die, and Person B, someone nearly attached to him—his mother or daughter or fiancée—learns the fact at about the same time through a visual or auditory perception. In this latter case, then, it is as if she had been informed by telephone, though such was not the case." Freud, *New Introductory Lectures on Psycho-Analysis,* in the *The Standard Edition of the Complete Psychological Works of Sigmund Freud* (*SE*) (London: Hogarth Press, 1974), 22:36. See also Peter

Szendy, *Phantom Limbs: On Musical Bodies*, trans. Will Bishop (New York: Fordham University Press, 2015).

28. Theodor W. Adorno, "Über die musikalische Verwendung des Radios," in *Der getreue Korrepetitor, Der getreue Korrepetitor: Lehrschriften zur musikalischen Praxis, Gesammelte Schriften*, 15:385.

29. As I was correcting the proofs of the French edition of these pages, I received the French translation of Avital Ronell's marvelous *The Telephone Book: Technology, Schizophrenia, Electric Speech* (Lincoln: University of Nebraska Press, 1989). Rereading it in my own language, I discover in it several motifs following the same thread that I have been pursuing here, to which it is impossible for me to do justice in a footnote. Therefore, for the time being, I leave this connection deferred.

30. Gaston Leroux, *The Phantom of the Opera*, trans. David Coward (Oxford: Oxford University Press, 2012), It appeared serially in *Le Gaulois*. The novel was first published as a book in 1911.

31. Ibid., 131.

32. Ibid., 134.

33. Ibid., 8.

34. Ibid., 51.

35. Ibid., 105.

36. Ibid., 238–39.

37. Ibid., 239.

38. Ibid., 81. Translation modified.

39. For more on *claqueurs* and the institution of the *claque* in nineteenth-century theaters, see Peter Szendy, *Listen: A History of Our Ears*, trans. Charlotte Mandell (New York: Fordham University Press, 2008), 112.

40. Leroux, *Phantom of the Opera*, 81, 83.

41. Ibid., 84. Translation modified.

42. Ibid., 84–85.

43. Ibid., 87. Translation modified.

44. [Translator's note: The expression *coup de point* will take on special significance later. The French expression *coup de fil* means "phone call," so the image of the *coup de point* evokes in place of a "phone line" something like a "phone point" or, in the present context, a "dotted phone line."]

45. [Translator's note: The term "phonogroove" translates here *phonogriffure*. Szendy's terms *phonogriffe* and *phonogriffure* are puns on

phonographe and *phonogravure*. In this slight adjustment, phonic writing (*graphe*) becomes a scratch (*griffe*).]

46. Laurence Knapp, *Brian De Palma: Interviews* (Jackson: University Press of Mississippi, 2003), 10.

47. As Maurice Merleau-Ponty put it in "Blindness (*punctum caecum*) of 'consciousness,'" his working notes from May 1960: "The retina is blind at the point where the fibers that will permit the vision spread out into it." See Maurice Merleau-Ponty, *The Visible and the Invisible: Followed by Working Notes*, trans. Alfonso Lingis (Evanston, Ill.: Northwestern University Press, 1968), 248. Jacques Derrida picks up and analyzes these notes in *Memoirs of the Blind*, where he suggests that "at its originary point, the *trait* is invisible and the draftsman is blind to it." See Jacques Derrida, *Memoirs of the Blind: The Self-Portrait and Other Ruins*, trans. Pascale-Anne Brault and Michael Naas (Chicago: University of Chicago Press, 1993), 53.

48. See Peter Szendy and Nicolas Donin, "Otographes," *Circuit* 13, no. 2 (2003): 11–26.

49. [Translator's Note: Gainsbourg's song (whose refrain is "I make holes, little holes, still more little holes, / I make holes, little holes, always little holes") is sung by a desperate ticket puncher, ignored by everyone, who works in a little hole, punches tickets the whole day, and by the end of the song thinks about putting a hole into his own head.]

50. The term "exappropriation" was coined by Derrida: "In order for 'this' to make sense, I must be able, for example, to repeat, even if only virtually, I must be able by virtue of this iterability to appropriate: to see what I see, to get closer, to begin to identify, to recognize, in the broadest sense of these words—these are all processes of appropriation in the broadest sense. There is meaning only on this condition. But by the same token, there is meaning only insofar as this process of appropriation is, in advance, held in check or threatened by failure, virtually forbidden, limited, finite: meaning does not depend on me, it is what I will never be able to reappropriate totally. And what I call 'exappropriation' is this double movement in which I head toward meaning while trying to appropriate it, but while knowing at the same time that it remains—and while desiring, whether I realize it or not, that it remain—foreign, transcendent, other, that it stay where there is alterity." See Jacques Derrida and

Bernard Stiegler, *Echographies of Television*, trans. Jennifer Bajorek (Cambridge: Polity, 2002), 110–11.

51. I am, of course, thinking of *Scarface* here, the film that De Palma directed in 1983 with Al Pacino in the role of Tony Montana, the drug dealer with a scar.

52. In *Listen*, I proposed the idea that the digital bookmarking of a recording (what I called "track marks") was also a form of scansion comparable to the claque. Furthermore, this scansion of music through the means of organized applause appears to have been based on annotation: "Sometimes manuscripts, on which the passages that should be applauded are indicated in the margins, are given to the leaders of the claque," as we can read in the surprising work *Mémoires d'un claqueur* (Paris, 1829). Quoted in Szendy, *Listen*, 116.

53. Among the many interpreters of *Wozzeck*, George Perle (whose remarkable analysis I follow here) is to my knowledge the only one to have raised this question. See George Perle, *The Operas of Alban Berg* (Berkeley: University of California Press, 1980), 1:87.

54. *Unkenrufe*, as Berg put it on his piano-vocal score (m. 302).

55. "The cessation of the chromatically ascending progression at m. 302 and the return of the 'nature music' of the first part of the movement (mm. 226ff.), representing the croaking of the toads, marks the ultimate extinction of Wozzeck's life." Perle, *Operas of Alban Berg*, 2:123.

56. [Translator's Note: Szendy quotes here Pierre-Jean Jouve's French translations. See Pierre-Jean Jouve and Michel Fano, *Wozzeck d'Alban Berg* (Paris: Bourgois, 1985), 265. In order to maintain the continuity of Szendy's argument, I translate the French text into English here with an eye on the German original.]

57. In a completely different context and genre, we could think of the death of Mélisande, that also escaped the attention of those who surrounded her. At the conclusion of Debussy's *Pelléas et Mélisande* (in the fifth act), Arkel sings: "I heard nothing. So quickly. So quickly. She is gone without saying a word."

58. The exchange of voices does not stop between Wozzeck and the toads, as the voice of the toads is substituted for in Büchner's text by insects whose buzzing resembles cracked bells (*das Summen der Käfer wie gesprungene Glocken*). See Perle, *Operas of Alban Berg*, 2:86.

59. Following Heinrich Besseler's history of listening in the age of modernity, we could interpret this drowning as a staging of the completion or the closure of a certain auditory regime (a conclusion that is similar to my analysis of *Don Giovanni* that I put forth in *Listen*). But Besseler, when he turns the figure of immersion into the "passive listening of the Romantics" (whose aquatic paradigm is hence the prelude to Wagner's *The Rhine Gold*), proposes a broad periodization, to say the least. See the fifth chapter and the confrontation between Wagner and Nietzsche, who in *Human, All Too Human* (II, 134) speaks of a musical movement in terms of swimming. See Heinrich Besseler, *Das musikalische Hören der Neuzeit* (Berlin: Academie-Verlag, 1959). Also Szendy, *Listen*, 129.

60. Jacques Derrida, *The Animal That Therefore I Am*, trans. David Wills (New York: Fordham University Press, 2008), 11. It was for the same conference at Cerisy-la-Salle in June 1997 that I outlined this reading of Wozzeck's death. See my "Musicanimalités (*Experimentum phonocriticum*," in *L'Animal autobiographique: Autour de Jacques Derrida* (Paris: Galilée, 1999), 416.

61. Derrida, *The Animal That Therefore I Am*, 12, 11, 51.

62. Theodor W. Adorno and Walter Benjamin, *The Complete Correspondence, 1928–1940*, ed. Henri Lonitz (Cambridge, Mass.: Harvard University Press, 1999), 205.

63. "You know that whenever we talked about music, a field otherwise fairly remote from my own, it was only really when his work was under discussion that we reached the same level of intensity as we usually do in our discussions on other subjects. You will certainly still remember the conversation we had following a performance of *Wozzeck*." Ibid., 119.

64. With regard to Benjamin and the question of the detail, I can merely allude here in passing to his *The Origin of German Tragic Drama*, trans. John Osborne (New York: Verso, 2009). [Translator's note: The French word *détaillant* also means "retailer" in English.]

65. Arnold Schoenberg, "Letters to the Editor: 'Doctor Faustus' Schoenberg," in *Saturday Review of Literature* 32 (January 1, 1949): 22.

66. Theodore W. Adorno and Thomas Mann, *Correspondence, 1943–1955*, ed. Henri Lonitz (Cambridge: Polity, 2006), 13, emphasis in original.

67. See Stefan Müller-Doohm, *Adorno, une biographie*, trans. Bernard Lortholary (Paris: Gallimard, 2004), 319.

68. The expression "montage technique" can be found in Thomas Mann, *The Story of a Novel: The Genesis of Doctor Faustus*, trans. Richard Winston and Clara Winston (New York: Knopf, 1961), 32. For the quotation, see ibid., 34. See also Mann's first letter to Adorno on October 5, 1943, as well as the letter from December 30, 1945. Adorno and Mann, *Correspondence*, 3, 12. Every time the question of montage appears in connection with the "details" that Mann says he needs for his book.

69. Theodor W. Adorno, "Die gewürdigte Musik," in *Der getreue Korrepetitor: Lehrschriften zur musikalischen Praxis, Gesammelte Schriften* (1963; Frankfurt: Suhrkamp, 1976), 15:184.

70. Theodor W. Adorno, "Anweisungen zum Hören neuer Musik" and "Über die musikalische Verwendung des Radios," in *Der getreue Korrepetitor: Lehrschriften zur musikalischen Praxis, Gesammelte Schriften*, 15:188–248, 369–401.

71. Adorno, *Der getreue Korrepetitor*, 159.

72. Adorno, "Über die musikalische Verwendung des Radios," 376.

73. Adorno, "Anweisungen zum Hören neuer Musik," 245.

74. Theodor W. Adorno, "Schöne Stellen," in *Musikalische Schriften V, Gesammelte Schriften* (Frankfurt: Suhrkamp, 1984), 18:695. I commented on this radio program in "S'arranger—de la phonographie," in *Musica practica* (Paris: L'Harmattan, 1997).

75. Adorno, "Schöne Stellen."

76. Adorno, "Über die musikalische Verwendung des Radios," 383.

77. Ibid., 385.

78. Adorno, "Schöne Stellen," 699–700.

79. Ibid., 700.

80. In his sketches, Adorno imagined a violin concerto by the diabolical composer that included a citation from Tartini's sonata "The Devil's Trill." For his cantata, he imagined an allusion either to "Lasciatemi morire" from Monteverdi's *Lamento d'Arianna* or to Peri and Caccini's *Orfeo*. For the same cantata, we find in these notes the following directions: "the chorus gradually introducing a symphonic movement, reversing, as it were, the Ode to Joy, just as Adrian saw his task to lie in repudiating the Ninth Symphony." See Adorno and Mann, *Correspondence*, 124.

81. During our first meeting (which took place, I believe, at the Lutétia in 1995), Jacques Derrida—the one whom these pages would like to

pay tribute to—confided to me with an inimitable and indecipherable smile: "Some of my friends tell me that I am like Adorno."

Exit: J.D.'s Dream

1. Jorge Luis Borges, "The Garden of Forking Paths," in *Labyrinths: Selected Stories and Other Writings*, ed. Donald A. Yates and James E. Irby (New York: New Directions, 2007), 19.
2. Ibid.
3. Jacques Derrida, *The Post Card: From Socrates to Freud and Beyond*, trans. Alan Bass (Chicago: University of Chicago Press, 1987), 19.
4. Ibid., 20.
5. Jacques Derrida and Marie-Françoise Plissart, *Right of Inspection*, trans. David Wills (New York: Monacelli Press, 1998), 124.
6. It is "in a blowup, in a process of increasing enlargement, of *découpage* or montage" that "the significant 'detail'" becomes legible. And "Nothing escapes the 'magnifier,' since there is only detail." Ibid., 125.
7. "The effect of the whole is always seen reinserted within a part, which is enlarged more than everything else." Ibid., 125.
8. I will highlight, in passing, another one of these avatars that transposes the blowup into the auditory field: Jack (John Travolta), the sound engineer in Brian De Palma's remarkable *Blow Out*, which is a kind of remake of Antonioni's *Blow-Up*. (I analyzed this film in "*Blow Out* ou la captation.")
9. "General theory," Derrida writes, is "another name for the panoptical" (Derrida and Plissart, *Right of Inspection*, 126). Or "There is no right to a complete inspection [*regard total*], it is the opposite of a panopticon" (125).
10. Ibid., 129.
11. Ibid., 130.
12. Derrida, *Post Card*, 19.
13. The playful word "dichemination" appears in *The Post Card*, page 142. [Translator's note: The English translation of *The Post Card* uses the French term "dichemination." The word is actually a pun on "dissemination" and means something like "derailment."] (He confided to me once that he had abandoned "a long time ago" the plan to write something about Stravinsky.)

14. Jacques Derrida, "Cette nuit dans la nuit de la nuit . . ." [a reading of Marie-Louise Mallet's *La Musique en respect* (Paris: Galilee, 2002)] in *Rue Descartes* 42, 124–25. An outline or a first version of this dream can be found in Jacques Derrida and Geoffrey Bennington, *Jacques Derrida* (Chicago: University of Chicago Press, 1993), 208.

15. Derrida and Bennington, *Jacques Derrida*, 24.

16. Derrida, *Post Card*, 120. We find here a structure quite close to what I have called elsewhere "retroprospection" or "retroprophecy." See Peter Szendy, *Prophecies of Leviathan: Reading Past Melville*, trans. Gil Anidjar (New York: Fordham University Press, 2010).

17. Such were his (posthumous) last words read at the cemetery of Ris-Orangis on October 12, 2004. See Jacques Derrida, "Final Words," trans. Gila Walker, *Critical Inquiry* 33, no. 2 (Winter 2007): 462.

18. Derrida and Bennington, *Jacques Derrida*, 39–40.

19. Derrida, "Cette nuit dans la nuit de la nuit," 124.

20. As a kind of dialogue inside the ear, in short, such as Nietzsche staged it in his striking "Conversation on Music" (in *Daybreak*, #255). I put forward a reading of this text in "Conversation secrète," *Vacarme* 37 (October 11, 2006): http://www.vacarme.org/article1192 .html.

21. [Translator's note: Once again, Szendy combines here "topologie" with the French word "taupe" which means "mole." Thus, "taupologie" is something like the topology of moles or even a topology that is already undermined and burrowed by secret agents.]

BIBLIOGRAPHY

Adorno, Theodor W. *Der getreue Korrepetitor: Lehrschriften zur musikalischen Praxis, Gesammelte Schriften.* Vol. 15. Frankfurt: Suhrkamp, 1976.

———. *Introduction to the Sociology of Music.* Translated by E. B. Ashton. New York: Seabury Press, 1976.

———. *Musikalische Schriften V, Gesammelte Schrifte.* Vol. 18. Frankfurt: Suhrkamp, 1984.

Adorno, Theodor W., and Walter Benjamin. *The Complete Correspondence, 1928–1940.* Edited by Henri Lonitz. Cambridge, Mass.: Harvard University Press, 1999.

Adorno, Theodor W., and Thomas Mann. *Correspondence, 1943–1955.* Edited by Henri Lonitz. Cambridge: Polity, 2006.

Allanbrook, Wye Jamison. *Rhythmic Gesture in Mozart: Le Nozze di Figaro and Don Giovanni.* Chicago: University of Chicago Press, 1983.

Anidjar, Gil. *"Our Place in al-Andalus": Kabbalah, Philosophy, Literature in Arab Jewish Letters.* Stanford: Stanford University Press, 2002.

Barthes, Roland. "Listening." In *The Responsibility of Forms: Critical Essays on Music, Art, and Representation*, translated by Richard Howard, 245–60. Berkeley: University of California Press, 1991.

Beaumarchais, Pierre-Augustin Caron de. *The Figaro Trilogy: The Barber of Seville, The Marriage of Figaro, The Guilty Mother.* Translated by David Coward. Oxford: Oxford University Press, 2008.

Benjamin, Walter. *The Origin of German Tragic Drama.* Translated by John Osborne. New York: Verso, 2009.

————. "(Tele)Pathie." In *Gesammelte Schriften*, edited by Rolf Tiedemann and Hermann Schweppenhauser, 6:187–88. Frankfurt: Suhrkamp, 1991.

Bentham, Jeremy. *The Panopticon Writings*. New York: Verso, 2011.

Besseler, Heinrich. *Das musikalische Hören der Neuzeit*. Berlin: Academie-Verlag, 1959.

Borges, Jorge Luis. *Labyrinths: Selected Stories and Other Writings*. Edited by Donald A. Yates and James E. Irby. New Directions, 2007.

Calvino, Italo. *Under the Jaguar Sun*. Translated by William Weaver. New York: Harcourt Brace, 1990.

Campbell, Duncan. *Surveillance électronique planétaire*. Paris: Allia, 2001.

Cerchiari, Luca. *Jazz e fascism*. Palermo: L'Epos, 2003.

Chion, Michel. *Film, a Sound Art*. Translated by Claudia Gorbman. New York: Columbia University Press, 2009.

Cortázar, Julio. *Blow-Up and Other Stories*. Translated by Paul Blackburn. New York: Collier, 1963.

Da Ponte, Lorenzo. *Memoirs*. Translated by Elisabeth Abbott. New York: New York Review of Books, 2000.

Deleuze, Gilles. "Postscript on Societies of Control." In *Negotiations*, translated by Martin Joughin. 177–82. New York: Columbia University Press, 1997.

Derrida, Jacques. *The Animal That Therefore I Am*. Translated by David Will. New York: Fordham University Press, 2008.

————. "Cette nuit dans la nuit de la nuit." *Rue Descartes* 42 (2003): 112–27.

————. "Faith and Knowledge: The Two Sources of 'Religion' at the Limits of Reason." In *Acts of Religion*, edited by Gil Anidjar, 42–101. New York: Routledge, 2002.

————. "Final Words." Translated by Gila Walker. *Critical Inquiry* 33, no. 2 (Winter 2007): 462.

————. *Memoirs of the Blind: The Self-Portrait and Other Ruins*. Translated by Pascale-Anne Brault and Michael Naas. Chicago: University of Chicago Press, 1993.

————. *The Post Card: From Socrates to Freud and Beyond*. Translated by Alan Bass. Chicago: University of Chicago Press, 1987.

————. *Rogues: Two Essays on Reason*. Translated by Pascale-Anne Brault and Michael Naas. Stanford: Stanford University Press, 2005.

Derrida, Jacques, and Geoffrey Bennington. *Jacques Derrida*. Chicago: University of Chicago Press, 1993.

Derrida, Jacques, and Marie-Françoise Plissart. *Right of Inspection*. Translated by David Wills. New York: Monacelli Press, 1998.

Derrida, Jacques, and Bernard Stiegler. *Echographies of Television*. Translated by Jennifer Bajorek. Cambridge: Polity, 2002.

Dümling, Albrecht, and Peter Girth. *Entartete Musik: Eine kommentierte Rekonstruktion*. Düsseldorf: Der Kleine Verlag, 1988.

Dumont, Étienne. *Mémoire sur un nouveau principe pour construire des maisons d'inspection, et nommément des maisons de force*. Paris: Mille et une nuits, 2002.

Eco, Umberto. "L'Anopticon." In *Il secondo diario minimo*. Milan: Bompiani, 1992.

Eugène, Jean-Pierre. *La Musique dans les films d'Alfred Hitchcock*. Paris: Dreamland, 2000.

Ferguson, Russell. "The Variety of Din." In *Christian Marclay*, 19–58. Los Angeles: UCLA Hammer Museum, 2003.

Foucault, Michel. *Discipline and Punish: The Birth of the Prison*. Translated by Alan Sheridan. New York: Vintage, 1995.

———. *The Order of Things: An Archaeology of the Human Sciences*. New York: Routledge, 2005.

Freud, Sigmund. "A Case of Paranoia Running Counter to the Psycho-Analytic Theory of the Disease." In *The Standard Edition of the Complete Psychological Works of Sigmund Freud*, translated and edited by James Strachey, 14:263–72. London: Hogarth, 1961.

———. *New Introductory Lectures on Psycho-Analysis*. In *The Standard Edition of the Complete Psychological Works of Sigmund Freud*, translated and edited by James Strachey. Vol. 22. London: Hogarth, 1965.

———. "On the Grounds for Detaching a Particular Syndrome from Neurasthenia under the Description 'Anxiety Neurosis.'" In *The Standard Edition of the Complete Psychological Works of Sigmund Freud*, translated and edited by James Strachey, 3:87–115. London: Hogarth Press, 1962.

Furtwängler, Wilhelm. "Bach." In *Furtwängler on Music*, translated by Ronald Taylor, 27–28. Hants: Scolar Press, 1991.

———. "Bach." In *Ton und Wort: Aufsätze und Vorträge, 1918 bis 1954*, 214–20. Wiesbaden: F. A. Brockhaus, 1958.

————. "Heinrich Schenker: A Contemporary Problem." *Sonus* 6, no. 1 (1985): 4–5.

————. *Notebooks, 1924–1954*. Translated by Shaun Whiteside. New York: Quartet Books, 1989.

Gronda, Giovanna, and Paolo Fabbri. *Libretti d'opera italiani, dal Seicento al Novecento*. Milan: Monadori, 1997.

Hegel, Georg Wilhelm Friedrich. *Aesthetics: Lectures on Fine Art*. Vol. 2. Translated by T. M. Knox. Oxford: Oxford University Press, 1998.

The Holy Bible: New Revised Standard Version with Apocrypha. New York: Oxford University Press, 1989.

Hughes, David. *The Complete Lynch*. London: Virgin Books, 2001.

Jouve, Pierre-Jean, and Michel Fano. *Wozzeck d'Alban Berg*. Paris: Bourgois, 1985.

Joyce, James. *Finnegans Wake*. New York: Penguin, 1976.

Kafka, Franz. *The Complete Stories*. Edited by Nahum N. Glatzer. New York: Schocken, 1972.

Kant, Immanuel. *Critique of the Power of Judgment*. Translated by Paul Guyer. Cambridge: Cambridge University Press, 2001.

Kircher, Athanasius. *Musurgia universalis*. Vol. 2. Rome, 1650.

Knapp, Laurence. *Brian De Palma: Interviews*. Jackson: University Press of Mississippi, 2003.

Lauxerois, Jean. "'À bon entendeur': Petite note sur l'écoute structurelle." *Circuit* 14, no. 1 (2003): 87–102.

Leroux, Gaston. *The Phantom of the Opera*. Translated by David Coward. Oxford: Oxford University Press, 2012.

"Les grandes oreilles de Tony Blair: La polémique sur les écoutes visant Kofi Annan." *Libération*, February 28–29, 2004.

Levin, Thomas. "Rhetoric of the Temporal Index: Surveillant Narration and the Cinema of 'Real Time.'" In *CTRL [Space]: Rhetorics of Surveillance from Bentham to Big Brother*, edited by Thomas Levin, Ursula Frohne, and Peter Weibel, 578–93. Cambridge: MIT Press, 2002.

Mann, Thomas. *The Story of a Novel: The Genesis of Doctor Faustus*. Translated by Richard Winston and Clara Winston. New York: Knopf, 1961.

Melton, H. Keith. *The Ultimate Spy Book*. New York: Dorling Kindersley, 1996.

Merleau-Ponty, Maurice. *The Visible and the Invisible: Followed by Working Notes*. Translated by Alfonso Lingis Evanston, Ill.: Northwestern University Press, 1968.

Müller-Doohm, Stefan. *Adorno, une biographie*. Translated by Bernard Lortholary. Paris: Gallimard, 2004.

Nancy, Jean-Luc. *Listening*. Translated by Charlotte Mandell. New York: Fordham University Press, 2007.

Nietzsche, Friedrich. *Daybreak: Thoughts on the Prejudices of Morality*. Edited by Maudemarie Clark and Brian Leiter. Cambridge: Cambridge University Press, 1997.

Pagé, Suzanne, Franck Popper, and René Block. *Écouter par les yeux: Objets et environnements sonores*. Paris: Musée d'Art Moderne, 1980.

Perle, George. *The Operas of Alban Berg*. Vol. 1. Berkeley: University of California Press, 1980.

Porta, John Baptista. *Natural Magick*. London: Thomas Young and Samuel Speed, 1658.

Rimbaud, Robin. "Scanner: Cartographier les villes." In *Sonic Process: Une nouvelle géographie des sons*, edited by Christophe Kihm, 240–45. Paris: Centre Pompidou, 2002.

Ronell, Avital. *The Telephone Book: Technology, Schizophrenia, Electric Speech*. Lincoln: University of Nebraska Press, 1989.

Schoenberg, Arnold. "Letters to the Editor: 'Doctor Faustus' Schoenberg." In *Saturday Review of Literature* 32 (January 1, 1949): 22.

Schwartz, Arthuro. *The Complete Works of Marcel Duchamp*. New York: Thames and Hudson, 1969.

Simon, François-René. "Le Monde selon Wayne." *Jazz Magazine* 544 (January 2004): 16–21.

Sophocles. *Les Limiers*. Translated by Paul Masqueray. Paris: Les Belles Lettres, 1934.

———. *Sophocles II: Ajax, The Women of Trachis, Electra, Philoctetes, The Trackers*. Translated by Mark Griffith, Glenn W. Most, David Grene, Richmond Lattimore. Chicago: University of Chicago Press, 2013.

Stevens, Denis. *L'Orfeo, favola in musica da Claudio Monteverde*. London: Novello, 1968.

Sun Tzu. *The Art of War*. Translated by Samuel B. Griffith. New York: Oxford University Press, 1971.

————. *L'Art de la guerre*. Translated by Jean Lévi. Paris: Hachette Littératures, 2000.

Swinburne, Henry. *Travels in the Two Sicilies, in the Years 1777, 1778,
1779, and 1780*. London: T. Cadell & P. Elmsky, 1790.

Szendy, Peter. "*Blow Out* ou la captation." *Vacarme* 36 (July 2, 2006):
http://www.vacarme.org/article685.html.

————. "Conversation secrète." *Vacarme* 37 (October 11, 2006): http://
www.vacarme.org/article1192.html.

————. *Listen: A History of Our Ears*. Translated by Charlotte Mandell.
New York: Fordham University Press, 2008.

————. "Musicanimalités (*Experimentum phonocriticum*)." In *L'Animal
autobiographique: Autour de Jacques Derrida*, edited by Marie-Louise
Mallet, 401–23. Paris: Galilée, 1999.

————. *Musica practica: Arrangements et phonographies de Monteverdi
a James Brown*. Paris: Harmattan, 1997.

Szendy, Peter, and Nicolas Donin. "Otographes." *Circuit* 13, no. 2 (2003):
11–26.

Truffaut, François. *Hitchcock*. New York: Simon and Schuster, 1967.

Zbikowski, Dörte. "The Listening Ear: Phenomena of Acoustic Surveillance." In *CTRL [Space]: Rhetorics of Surveillance from Bentham
to Big Brother*, edited by Thomas Levin, 32–49. Cambridge: MIT
Press, 2002.